"Beginning and established scholars in biography, autobiography, autoethnography, and oral and life history will profit from Mulvihill and Swaminathan's trans-disciplinary commentary and analysis of life writing. Ably contextualizing theory and generalizing practice, the authors offer experienced and well-reasoned guidance to those who want to write competently researched, readable, and honest narratives. The strategically positioned research journal and sketchbook exercises make the book a highly usable text for life writing courses. My only regret is that *Critical Approaches to Life Writing Methods in Qualitative Research* was not published fifty years earlier when I began my career as an historian and biographer of education."

Gerald L. Gutek, *Professor Emeritus,*
Loyola University Chicago

"Thalia Mulvihill and Raji Swaminathan offer a great gift to those qualitative researchers entering the burgeoning field of life writing and educational biography. This primer guides the life writer into new research realms and, from their well-conceived metaphor of dreamscapes, permits the neophyte to embrace, understand, and rejoice in the adventure and freedom of blending detailed scholarly research with imaginative, thoughtful writing. With carefully constructed research activities, the reader begins *Critical Approaches to Life Writing Methods in Qualitative Research* with great interest and concludes with great knowledge, prepared to embark upon the journey and joy of life writing and biographical inquiry."

Craig Kridel, *E. S. Gambrell Professor of Educational Studies and*
Curator of the Museum of Education, University of South Carolina

"Mulvihill and Swaminathan masterfully situate life writing methods in the realm of theoretical, historical, and methodological underpinnings of qualitative research. They invite readers to the forest of complex life writing with invaluable resources, creative ideas, and inspiring suggestions that readers can savour when they embark their own journey of life writing. *Critical Approaches to Life Writing Methods in Qualitative Research* is a must-read that will serve as a safety net for those who are hankering for a quality guide to understanding the value of storytelling. This book makes a remarkable contribution to the field of narrative inquiry!"

Jeong-Hee Kim, *Professor of Curriculum Studies and*
Teacher Education, Texas Tech University

CRITICAL APPROACHES TO LIFE WRITING METHODS IN QUALITATIVE RESEARCH

Life writing projects have become part of the expanding field of qualitative research methods in recent years and advances in critical approaches are reshaping methodological pathways. *Critical Approaches to Life Writing Methods in Qualitative Research* gives researchers and students looking for a brief compendium to guide their methodological thinking a concise and working overview of how to approach and carry out different forms of life writing.

This practical book re-invigorates the conversation about the possibilities and innovative directions qualitative researchers can take when engaged in various forms of life writing, such as biography, autobiography, autoethnography, life history, and oral history. It equips the reader with the tools to carry out life writing projects from start to finish, including choosing a topic or subject, examining lives as living data, understanding the role of documents and artifacts, learning to tell the story, and finally writing/performing/displaying through the voice of the life writer. The authors also address the ways a researcher can begin a project, work through the issues they might face along the journey, and arrive at a shareable product.

With its focus on the plurality of life writing methodologies, *Critical Approaches to Life Writing Methods in Qualitative Research* occupies a distinct place in qualitative research scholarship and offers practical exercises to guide the researcher. Examples include exploring authorial voice, practical applications of reflexivity exercises, the relationship between the narrator and participants, navigating the use of public and private archives, understanding the processes of collaborative inquiry and collaborative writing, and writing for various audiences.

Thalia M. Mulvihill, Ph.D., Professor of Social Foundations and Higher Education at Ball State University, serves as President of the International Society for Educational Biography and the Secretary for the AERA Biographical and Documentary Research SIG. Her areas of expertise include qualitative research methods, life writing, innovative pedagogies, history, and sociology of higher education.

Raji Swaminathan, Ph.D., is an Associate Professor in the Department of Educational Policy and Community Studies at the University of Wisconsin-Milwaukee. Her research and teaching interests are in the areas of emerging methods in qualitative research, urban education, and alternative education.

CRITICAL APPROACHES TO LIFE WRITING METHODS IN QUALITATIVE RESEARCH

Thalia M. Mulvihill and
Raji Swaminathan

Routledge
Taylor & Francis Group

NEW YORK AND LONDON

First published 2017
by Routledge
711 Third Avenue, New York, NY 10017

and by Routledge
2 Park Square, Milton Park, Abingdon, Oxon OX14 4RN

Routledge is an imprint of the Taylor & Francis Group, an informa business

British Library Cataloguing-in-Publication Data
A catalogue record for this book is available from the British Library

Library of Congress Cataloging-in-Publication Data
A catalog record has been requested

ISBN: 978-1-138-64300-0 (hbk)
ISBN: 978-1-138-64299-7 (pbk)
ISBN: 978-1-315-62958-2 (ebk)

Typeset in Bembo and ITC Stone Sans
by Apex CoVantage, LLC

CONTENTS

1

INTRODUCTION AND OVERVIEW

Qualitative researchers are storytellers. There are many ways to tell a story. Biographers, autobiographers, autoethnographers, life historians, and oral historians all engage in the process of storytelling through life writing. Our opening premise for this book is that storytelling matters; it matters to individuals, it matters to cultures and subcultures, and it matters to our individual and collective beings as we engage our imagination about past, present, and future human experiences. Critical approaches to all of these forms of life writing require certain preconditions for storytelling; namely, that the storyteller be mindful of the powerful agency vested in the meaning-making storyteller, who must also understand that they are a story-creator first before they are a storyteller. The motivations qualitative researchers have for creating stories, the tools life writers use, and the various containers and vessels they shape to hold and transport these stories are worthy of continued examination.

Life writing projects have evolved as part of the expanding field of qualitative research approaches and have benefitted from the method-ological musings of many scholars, which we will selectively highlight throughout the book. This book will introduce and discuss the similarities and distinctions between biography, autobiography, auto-ethnography, life history, and oral history approaches to life writing, as well as the arguments surrounding the often artificial boundaries between "fiction" and "non-fiction" in social science representations of life stories. Examples from each will be used to illustrate the exciting work being done within each of these approaches and prepare the reader for the intellectual challenges and questions that life writing projects entail. We hope that as you contemplate your own life writing projects, you will find companionship within these pages and that you will revel in the possibilities for multiple pathways for creating and telling stories of lasting meaning using qualitative inquiry traditions, approaches, and tools.

Life writing projects have become part of the expanding field of qualitative research methods in recent years. In the last decade, biography and autobiographical genres have expanded to include autoethnography (Carolyn Ellis, Laurel Richardson, Stacy Holman Jones, and Tony Adams), duoethnography, oral history (Groundswell organization), radio and podcast productions (Murder, Someone Knows Something, and Serial), illustrated biographies (Zena Alkayat and Nina Cosford), performance ethnography (Tami Spry), theatrical performances drawn from interview transcripts (Anna Deavere Smith), and various other forms of innovative life writing. This book examines the different ways in which critical auto/biographical methods can enhance and elevate life writing projects by closely examining innovative approaches used in narrating critical life writing. This close examination provides researchers with:

a. New methodological tools;
b. A review and discussion of scholars' approaches to life writing projects;
c. Guiding questions/prompts to help identify and learn to construct questions for each type of project;
d. Ways to develop and write a life writing project, distinguishing among the array of types of life writing projects; and
e. References to help further guide novice life writers.

Our intent in writing this book is to examine five different approaches to life writing—biography, autobiography, autoethnography, life history, and oral history—and compare them side by side so that we can see their similarities and differences. We do this by exploring how they are used in the usual and standard process of research, viz. starting with the research topic, research questions, data collection, data analysis, and writing up (or otherwise representing) the findings. We include the issues and dilemmas for each type of life writing approach, and some suggestions for evaluating them. We also address some blended versions, mashups, and/or extensions of these five approaches; for example, biography and autobiography have functioned as root and predominant categories. Collective biography can be understood as a methodological mashup between biography and qualitative inquiry in much the same way that collective autoethnography can be a methodological mashup between auto/biography and ethnography. And, using the arts to both create and communicate life writing projects can be extensions of these categories.

In putting together a book that is focused on different approaches to life writing, we wish to acknowledge the diversity in the field while presenting, in one place, a set of navigational tools. While the field of life writing is vast, we were drawn towards those research approaches to life writing that are most often used by students using the social sciences and novice qualitative researchers. We have included the often cited literature about life writing that we feel may be beneficial to qualitative researchers as well as additional writings that might help expand the range of possibilities for thinking about life writing projects. We hope that this book will provide those interested in life writing with a sense of how to conduct research within these approaches, how these particular approaches may differ from each other, and how to best determine the level of appropriateness when selecting an approach for a project, while at the same time encouraging methodological experimentation.

We direct this book towards students or novice researchers who have little or some knowledge of qualitative research and would now like to get a grasp of the diversity within life writing methods while also gaining an understanding of the overall research process. We write for those who are interested in starting a life writing project and would like a map of the territory to find their way into writing. We also write for our peers in academia who are from different disciplines (sociology, anthropology, history, geography, humanities, arts) and all those who seek to decolonize the writing of lives, who are advocates for hearing and learning from the messy stories of human beings. We write for those who are not content with telling human stories from a singular perspective.

Nesting Approaches to Life Writing within Critical Qualitative Research

We use the term "life writing" as an umbrella term to encompass a range of writing about lives, including but not limited to autobiography, biography, oral history, life history, autoethnography. While we touch on genres such as memoir, digital diaries, obituaries, or autobiographfiction, we do so to the extent that they emerge from the five categories we have chosen to expand in this book. We acknowledge that these distinctions and categories are not cast in stone. The blurring of distinctions between types of life writing has grown alongside a more general acceptance of life writing as a field of study. Neat categories fall apart when life writers reflect on the complexity of the lives they seek to represent and, instead of a chronological voice, what emerges is pluralistic, gloriously messy, multivoiced, and enhanced by the frames of critical theory.

Critical Approaches Signify a Value System

By the term "critical," we mean the capacity to interrogate and inquire against the grain. It means to ask questions that confront prevailing assumptions leading to an analysis, dismantling and uncovering omissions and invisibilities. A critical approach propels us toward a more nuanced understanding of intersectionality of identity constructions and reminds us that the way in which we construct life events/experiences and narrate or perform our interpretations can create the conditions for positive social change. Denzin and Giardina describe critical scholars as those

> committed to showing how the practices of critical, interpretive, qualitative research can help change the world in positive ways. They are committed to creating new ways of making the

practices of critical qualitative inquiry central to the workings of a free democratic society.

(Denzin and Giardina, 2013, p. 41)

A free democratic society is dependent upon bringing to fruition a vibrant notion of pluralism, both in thinking and in human interaction, and therefore qualitative researchers, taking up a critical approach, must be prepared to design knowledge-quests (i.e., qualitative inquiry projects) with the supposition that encouraging pluralistic thinking and knowing is valuable and essential.

To help situate researchers into the mindset of a critical life writer, we offer a series of research journal (RJ) and sketchbook (SB) exercises throughout the book. The first, below, illustrates the centrality of stories in our lives and why life writing requires us to listen to more than a single story.

Research Journal and Sketchbook Exercise 1

1. View the following TED Talk by Chimamanda Ngozi Adichie, *The Danger of a Single Story* (https://www.ted.com/talks/ chimamanda_adichie_the_danger_of_a_single_story? language=en), and write a page or two about what the title *The Danger of a Single Story* means to you in the context of life writing.
2. Next, find a postcard (of anything!) and paste it in your sketchbook.
3. Now imagine a person or a group of people who might inhabit the place or circumstance depicted on the postcard and write a fictional vignette that seems interesting and plausible to you about the life or lives of those you imagined.
4. Next, write a second vignette that defies the assumptions you started with during the writing of your first vignette.
5. Finally, re-draw, or trace, or in some fashion create a new postcard within your sketchbook that is more representative of the life or lives you have described in each vignette.
6. In your journal, reflect on what you learned from this exercise about life writing approaches.

Exercises such as this provide life writers with opportunities to grow their capacity to understand and engage with critical life writing approaches. They make us aware of our assumptions and then challenge them. Through an imaginative retelling, we realize that several stories are possible if only we are aware of and set aside our own habitual ways of thinking. Life writing can be a way to understand the construction of the self, which encompasses the constructions of gender, race, culture, disability, sexuality, and ethnicity, among others such as place, nationality, and space. It involves issues of subjectivity, identity, and memory. It requires us to read so that we take into account truth, narrative and representation, and issues of power.

Critical Approaches Challenge the Status Quo

Critical approaches signify a value system. In this section, we take up the proposition that they also signify action. To understand what this means in the context of life writing research, we take up the challenge offered by critical scholars Cannella and Lincoln (2012) when they ask: "What does a critical perspective mean for research issues and questions, for frames that construct data collection and analyses, and forms of interpretation and re-presentation?" (Cannella and Lincoln, 2012, p. 104). To put this question within a frame of critical action, we turn to Pasque, Carducci, Kuntz, and Gildersleeve (2012) in order to gather our thoughts around qualitative inquiry as a "radical democratic act" (p. 3) against inequities in higher education, and to Denzin's (2010) *Qualitative Manifesto: A Call to Arms*, where he insists that critical inquiry is a "form of activism, of critique" (p. 34). We consider these challenges and attitudes within the context of life writing with the following questions: What does a critical perspective mean for life writing projects? How can life writers consider the framing of their projects using critical approaches? We answer these questions throughout the book in our framing of life writing as a consciously critical act that opens up a creative process and leads us to see and understand the connections between a particular life and the human condition.

"Critical approaches" is the phrase we use to situate the range of actions life writers take when designing and carrying out projects that aim to challenge the status quo—to address and redress neoliberal conditions that often render many voices and life experiences to invisibility or misinterpretation. Neoliberalism, defined broadly, is a policy that targets institutions that usually lie outside the market to bring them inside the market through privatization, elimination, or closure, or through reinvention. Education and trade unions are two prime examples of institutions affected by neoliberal policies. The ethical and social values that undergird neoliberal policies are those of competition. The state, as an active force, helps to create conditions that promote competition that produces inequality (Davies, 2014). Neoliberal conditions often fail to take into account the experiences of individuals within groups so that, as Robert McChesney (1999) explained, "proponents of neoliberalism sound as if they are doing poor people, the environment and everyone else a tremendous service as they enact policies on behalf of the wealthy few" (McChesney, 1999, p. 8). Critical approaches within a life writing context challenge the neoliberal condition as status quo. For critical scholars, a Bakhtinian notion of "self" is more appropriate for life writing. Bakhtin's (1986; 1992) "self" is dialogically co-constructed and always historically contingent. The self is co-constructed through dialogue and works to preserve the different perspectives that it opens up. Bakhtin's theory applied to life writing projects helps us understand not only that the subject of the life writing project is co-constructed by the life writer and the reader, but also reminds us of the constructed nature of time, place, and meaning-making. For example, Marlene Kadar (1999; 2014) and Sandeep R. Singh (2016) drew similar connections where they defined critical life writing as a practice that is meant to engage the reader in the text in a Bakhtinian way. By this they mean that when life writers engage with their subjects dialogically, the self of the other is not an objectivized self, and is instead whole, and the reader is able to similarly engage with the text and with the experiences of the lives recorded. A Bakhtinian reading is a dialogic reading where the reader has a dialogue with the text. The sense of opening towards new vistas is possible when the life writer leaves the work of describing lives incomplete rather than entombing lives. In this sense, critical life writing practice tries to create gateways to new understandings, points us towards new and old sources in ways that create a deeper interpretation. The life writer is thus engaged less with crafting a life as an endpoint or as a postscript, or almost an entombment of a life, but instead remains in the realm of the "unfinished" in the Freirean sense of open to possibilities (Freire, 1970). The next exercise will help you to think about life writing as a creative act comprising many pieces that need to be put together. The different ways in which they can be arranged or crafted represents the different ways in which the story of a life can be told.

Research Journal and Sketchbook Exercise 2

1. Collage of a life (for your sketchbook): Think of a person whose life you would like to research. If possible, get an outline portrait of the person or draw an outline of the person in your sketchbook. Now fill it in and make a collage by using at least three different source materials. For example, you could use diary excerpts, timelines, pictures or photographs, published material. Use materials of different types and sources to illustrate the lived life of the person. Let your imagination take flight.

2. Collage of a life (journal reflection): Think about the process of sketching and making a collage of a life and reflect on the following questions in the journal portion of your sketchbook journal:
    *   How did the experience help you to construct the life? What did you learn from the collage-making of a life?
    *   What made you choose these particular source materials? What was left out?
    *   In what way is the process of life writing constraining and/or freeing?

Critical Life Writing as a Form of Social Action

Critical approaches to life writing not only consider life writing as a way to challenge the status quo by engaging the lives and voices of the marginalized, but critical life writers look upon life writing as a space or site for social critique and social action (Couser, 2005), and often take an intersectionality approach. One of the advantages of critical approaches to life writing is that it not only talks back to stereotypical depictions of oppressions, but opens a space for inter-sectional analyses and depictions that are complex. Intersectionality theories (Crenshaw, 1989) help elevate the possibilities for life writ-ers by contemplating ways intersecting aspects of one's identity can influence the lived experience. Using an intersectionality framework for life writing projects demands that the researcher guard against theoretically erasing aspects of their subject's, or their own, identity. Rather than setting up binary oppositions, analogous descriptions, or a hierarchy between positions (gender versus race, gender as race, gender subsumed within race), intersectional analysis moves away from such false separations and instead discusses how these inter-sect in lives in unique ways. The intersectional approach talks back to deficit-depictions of disability, gender, sexuality, and race while also resisting accepted social models of the same. Life writing that resists not only deficit-depictions but also accepted social models, as Ferri (2011) reiterates, should "not be seen as something to suppress but to embrace" (p. 2276). As life writers, our built categories for analysis and meaning-making must not follow tropes or rehearsed scripts, or be filled with reified concepts of human experience, but must follow the authentic lived experiences of those we are writ-ing about. We must challenge our a priori categories and dominant discourses when conveying a life and, in so doing, we elevate the possibility for life writing to be a form of social action. Our ability to do this as life writers is directly proportional to our ability to ask critical questions within qualitative inquiry projects (Swaminathan and Mulvihill, 2017), to reflexively challenge our assumptions (even the most comforting and seemingly logical), and to be willing to live within the pain, joy, confusion, surprise, frustration, delight, anguish, and grace of exploring the human condition.

Critical Approaches and the Sociological Imagination

Critical approaches move away from modes of writing that take a grand theory approach (C. Wright Mills, 1959) that organizes the telling of a life into pre-conceived scripts and instead attempts to both examine and write lives that are complex, flawed, and realistic. Life writing that aims to create awareness and serve as a catalyst for change can focus on themes that touch the broader social and political arena. It can complicate and illuminate the overlaps between the personal narrative and the social world, explicate the tensions between the two, and call attention to the invisibility of, or omissions in, the construction of narratives of trauma (Gilmore, 2001), disability (Couser, 2005; Sherry, 2005), colonization (Spivak, 1988), and many others.

An important assumption in life writing is that the subjective perceptions, views, and experiences of the writer shape reality. Life writers challenge the positivist idea of an objective reality or a fixed truth. Instead, they align with the paradigm that acknowledges multiple points of view and values personal voice and reflexivity. Valuing the inner subjective experiences of researchers means regarding the researcher or life writer as a "connoisseur" (Eisner, 1991). For Eisner, the eye of the researcher incorporated human qualities and values such as a frame of reference, intention, and purpose. The eye was not a mechanical device used to record everything, but being "enlightened" represented an educated awareness and a capability for nuances and multiple dimensions. In this sense, life writing not only records the world seen by the researcher, but more importantly, shows how the researcher made sense of that world.

Ten Propositions about Critical Approaches to Life Writing

We offer a series of ten brief propositions that are intended to give a snapshot of some of the key ideas contained in what we mean by "critical approaches" to life writing:

1. Critical approaches to life writing understand the constructed nature of the "self" (Bakhtin, 1986; 1992).
2. Critical approaches to life writing privilege and empower individuals to talk and write as critics of oppression. Life writers engage with concepts of voice, ethics, reflexivity, and the politics of representation.
3. Critical approaches to life writing engage with discourses, history, and ideologies to explain and contextualize a life (Kelly, 2013).

4. Critical approaches to life writing work against forms of division and compartmentalization as they create portraits of lives that are meaningful (Kadar, 1992).

5. Critical approaches encourage individuals to counter-narrate or tell counter stories that create meanings of their lives that challenge the dominant discourses of race and class or gender or disability (Solorzano and Yosso, 2002). Such approaches confront a singular, dominant understanding of social and political conditions surrounding a life.

6. Critical approaches resemble what other education literatures refer to as culturally responsive approaches. There are many resources to help grapple with the mindset and the actions that educators can take to forge more culturally responsive pedagogies (see for example the work of Gloria Ladson Billings, Geneva Gay, Tyrone Howard, and others). And in much the same way, researchers engaging in any form of life writing must be culturally responsive researchers willing and able to deeply investigate and understand the context within which a life is lived.

7. Critical life writing projects have the potential to elevate the interdisciplinary and transdisciplinary knowledge we have about people in meaningful ways, resulting in greater understanding and empathy for the human condition (Eagan and Helms, 2002; Baena, 2013).

8. Critical approaches to life writing often foster social justice lenses to be used when interpreting lives. A variety of perspectives are used to examine assumptions, analyze power dynamics as they are played out within particular contexts, and interrogate the processes of how narratives simultaneously make some aspects of the lived experience highly visible and other aspects interminably invisible.

9. Critical approaches are "messy." Life writers struggle with these choices and communicate their awareness of the consequences of their choices through a process of reflexivity. By engaging in reflexivity, life writers share their decision-making processes and interrogate their own position vis-à-vis the project with which they engage.

10. Critical approaches make possible the "compatibility of feminist and postcolonial critical practices" (Moore-Gilbert, 2009).

Life writing projects using critical approaches can transform the questions we are willing to ask about how lives are narrated, and by whom, as well as propel new understandings of the conditions that shape lives.

Historical Tracings of the Term "Life Writing"

"Life writing," the term, can be traced back to the 1800s. *The Penny Cyclopedia of the Society of the Diffusion of the Useful* (1835) defines the term "biography" as literally meaning life writing, originating in the Greek *bios* meaning "life" and *graphia* meaning "writing." Although the term life writing has been attributed to Virginia Woolf in her 1939 "A Sketch of the Past," the use of the term can be traced to much earlier writings. In 1815, we find an article that refers to biography as life writing in the magazine, *The Port Folio*, which started in 1801 and closed in 1827. References to life writing can be found in the *Idler* in 1837 in a letter to the editor that appeared in the *Idler or Breakfast Companion*, Saturday edition, July 15 1837, titled "How to write one's own life." Signed in Latin with *Ego, Ispe, Mei* (or "I, myself, me"), these short articles are satirical sketches that question the value of life writing and narrowly define it as writing for self-aggrandizement or self-promotion, a sentiment that can sometimes be encountered in the present day. Marilyn Zucker's (2015) account of the responses of students in Portugal as recently as 2010 in her class on life writing describes the resistance she initially faced with introducing life writing to her class. Initially explaining that "Portuguese people don't like calling attention to themselves" and that "the influence of the Church . . . wants us to be humble," they eventually saw that there was a story that could emerge from their experiences and that their personal lives mattered and had meaning for them and others. Life writing can run the risk of being seen as "too personal," a charge leveled, as we have seen, from the early days. The focus on the individual was seen as an emphasis that was at the cost of a broader understanding of the social and political contexts. Disability memoirs are a case in point, where scholars warn against reifying the script of the individual "overcoming" (Davis, 1995; Mitchell and Snyder, 2000; Mollow, 2002). The evolution of critical disability studies and how it has been applied—for example, to life writing (Couser, 2009; Singh, 2016)—have added measurably to our understanding of transgressive possibilities for life writing as a force for social action. If we trace historical influences on autobiography, we can go as far back as Augustine's *Confessions* (398 CE) or Rousseau's book of the same name (1782). These autobiographies focused on the act of reflexivity, inwardness, and self-interpretation (Peterson, 1986).

Historically the focus in life writing moved from an emphasis on an objective life to that of a fluid self that comes into existence with the writing so that both self and other are interwoven in the tapestry of the act of reflexivity, inwardness, and self-interpretation (Peterson, 1986).

When the term "life writing" itself remains wonderfully ambiguous and agile, allowing life writers to remain responsive to the intersectionality of the "self" and to conceptualize life writing projects as domains for deepening human understanding, the methodological innovations seem delightfully endless.

Typologies of Approaches to Life Writing

Several scholars classify life writing under the broader umbrella term "narrative related approaches" (Creswell, 2013). Creswell (2013) gives examples such as life history, autoethnography, and biography as types of narrative approaches. Life writing for Flick (2014) is part of a narrative interview or a biographical interview that is used to elicit biographical details of a person's life. Life history, autoethnography, and biography appear consistently in almost all narrative approaches to life writing. For example, let's consider the work of the following life writers:

Norman Denzin's (1989/2014) approach to biography and autoethnography are from the interpretive epistemological perspective. By introducing the concept of "epiphanies" (p. 43), or turning points in a person's life, he describes the work of life writers or researchers as looking for stories that have a "deep effect" or an "epiphany" in the life of the person. He focuses on how people give coherence to their narrations of their lives and the structures that are behind their narratives. Louis M. Smith's (1994; 2014) cross-pollination of genea-logical and biographical methods resulted in a rich series of reflexive essays about the research process as he welcomes his readers into the continuous journey of biographer as detective and the richness that can result when stories remain open and not prematurely closed.

Craig Kridel's (1998) *Writing Educational Biography* is a beautiful edited collection of chapters where life writers are grappling with differ-ent dimensions of educational biography. This collection appeared at the moment when biography was undergoing a renewal process as it was taken up by qualitative researchers within the broad field of education. The convergence of new methodological turns in qualitative inquiry and interdisciplinary approaches to biography gave rise to new method-ological questions. Judy Long (1999) moved the needle on expanding ways that sociological life history was conceptualized, resulting in new methodological thinking about the relational qualities of life writing with her Subject, Narrator, Reader, and Text (SNRT) concept.

Carolyn Heilbrun's (1988) contributions to feminist approaches to life writing were groundbreaking. In *Writing a Woman's Life* she com-municates with such verisimilitude the social and intellectual impact of centering narratives on men rather than women and the promising possibilities for all when women write with women's life experiences at the center. And her Amanda Cross series of mystery novels extols the virtues of writing fiction from a pseudonym, pushing the edges of a female protagonist, Kate Fansler, providing her a palette from which to make social commentary within another form of life writing. This represents autobiographication, a process where forms of life writing are used within fiction. May Sarton's lifelong experimentation across genre drove home the vast potential for different forms of life writ-ing and the powerful insights that can be shared about the human condition (Mulvihill, 2000). C. Wright Mills (1959) described the "sociological imagination" as the intersection of history and biogra-phy at a time when sociologists were grappling with the category of "sociological life history" and proclaimed that "no social study that does not come back to the problems of biography, history and of their intersections within a society has completed its intellectual journey" (p. 6). Inspired by these life writers, we selected five approaches to life writing, as explicated below.

Five Approaches to Life Writing

The following five approaches to life writing will each be described as related yet distinct:

1. Biography
2. Autobiography
3. Autoethnography
4. Life history
5. Oral history

Why We Chose These Five Approaches

Our choice was based on our experiences in using these approaches in our own research as well as guiding novice researchers through these qualitative inquiry projects that involve life writing approaches in the courses we teach and the doctoral students we mentor. A search of journals in the last five years found articles in different disciplines reflecting the increasing interest in these approaches (from disciplines such as health sciences, social work, sociology, anthropology, geography, humanities, and arts). In addition, we took into consideration approaches that have become increasingly popular as evidenced by the numbers of dissertations and panel presentations at conferences (ICQI, AERA QR-SIG, ISEB) within the last five years that used these life writing approaches. We highlight ways a researcher might begin thinking about and conducting research within each approach. While approaches to life writing tend to be genre blurring and tear down disciplinary walls such as anthropology or sociology, it is not our intention to rebuild these walls. Instead, we agree that all approaches have at their core stories or subjective accounts of people. They are descriptions, interpretations, and memories of living, both in the past and present, and cannot be compartmentalized easily into neat categories. Being and representing dynamic lives, they are also necessarily messy. As scholars explain, a common feature of all life writing and perhaps a reason for its continued popularity is that it allows human beings to understand and manage time (Ricoeur, 2010) and arrange events in sequence (Abbott, 2008).

Approaches tend to create a certain structure that is useful when embarking on a research project. And while we agree that approaches might seem like the redrawing of boundaries, we would like to think of these as dotted lines that can both blend and merge when needed and otherwise stay within their specific genres. Despite the boundary-crossing capacity of different life writing modes, each approach has a history, definitive features, procedures for research that best fit them that is distinct. For researchers new to life writing, we think that such a structure would prove useful. If life writing is considered the umbrella term under which life histories, oral histories, or autobiographies can be classified, it is also true that not all life histories are autobiographies and not all autobiographies are autoethnographies. For each approach, we present few source texts or works that are often cited. In addition, we refer to articles in journals and, finally, we point to some ways of thinking about these topics that we have arrived at through our own research into life writing projects.

Research Journal and Sketchbook Exercise 3

1. Think of the names of the five approaches we have out-lined above. What comes to your mind when you hear the following terms:
   a. Autobiography
   b. Autoethnography
   c. Biography
   d. Life history
   e. Oral history
      Write in your journal your own definitions of each term. If you take the example of your own life for life writing, how would each of the above approaches work? What do you think would distinguish one approach from another?
2. Draw or sketch a diagram that represents the differences or similarities in each of these approaches.
3. Reflect on what questions came to your mind as you were doing this exercise. Write those questions in your journal for later reference.

Next we move into questions that help examine the five approaches to life writing by using a framework to tease out distinctions between the approaches while solidifying an understanding of the root similarities.

Distinctions between Life History, Autobiography, Biography, Oral History, and Biography: *Who Tells the Story?*

This question, "Who tells the story?" is about identifying the narrator and is methodologically important—so important that it is essential for life writers to continually ask themselves this question. It reveals positionality; power dynamics; potential colonialist tendencies or practices; indications of a Western, Eastern, or indigenous notion of "self"; feminist or social justice desires; etc. These are often challenging aspects of life writing that are not always immediately clear to the researcher but must be continually interrogated in order for the essential reflexivity processes to positively impact the whole of the project.

When initially presented with the question "Who tells the story?" novice researchers might predictably respond in the following ways, yet these will soon reveal themselves as too simplistic once life writers are deeply engaged in the project:

Who tells the story in life history?

The participant shares the story with the researcher.

Who tells the story in autobiography?

The person whose story it is tells their own story.

Who tells the story in biography?

The researcher writes or tells the story of another person or persons (living or dead).

The Use of Metaphors in Life Writing

Lakoff and Johnson (2003/1980) define metaphors by explaining that "the essence of metaphor is understanding and experiencing one kind of thing in terms of another" (p. 125). According to Lakoff and Johnson (2003/1980), we tend to define our reality in terms of metaphors and then act on the basis of those metaphors. For example, if we look at writing as discipline, then expressions such as "You have to glue yourself to the seat" or "Writing is sitting at your desk and waiting for drops of blood to form on your forehead" also tell us that writing is agony. On the other hand, writing can be viewed as fun when we think of it as a journey or as painting a picture with words. Lakoff and Johnson (2003/1980) point out that metaphors are conceptual vehicles for understanding and that metaphors represent our use of imaginative rationality. Through metaphors, we can get partial pictures and understandings of concepts that cannot be grasped fully at one time. For example, metaphors are good tools to convey emotional states of being or aesthetic expressions or ethical practices. The work of Lakoff and Johnson (2003/1980) can be useful for life writers who need to be aware of the use of metaphors in life writing. Participants' descriptions of life events need to be understood both for content and by the metaphors used to describe the experience. Similarly, for the life writer, in telling the story, the metaphors used can uncover a second layer to the structure of meaning-making.

Fiction and Non-Fiction

Life writing challenges the presumed rigid boundaries between fiction and non-fiction. Leavy (2013a), for example, points out that in autoethnography and narrative writing, fiction and non-fiction blur boundaries, as researchers do more than record facts and fiction writers often ground their stories in facts. Leavy has produced a plethora of examples of how researchers can use social science data and create fictional composites (Leavy, 2013b; Leavy, 2015). J.M. Coetzee's *Summertime* (2010) is an example of a fictionalized biography that describes the story of a young biographer working on a biography of the "late" Coetzee. Rigid categories of fiction and non-fiction tend to blur in biographical writing. Biography, often considered a subcategory of historical writing, is frequently cast as non-fictional with a narrative structure involving the passage of time. However, like fiction, biographers try to narrate the inner emotions, feelings, and thoughts of their subjects as well as describe critical events and their subject's participation in those events. In doing so, biographers draw on some of the strategies used by fiction writers. To conclude Chapter 1, please consider the following prompts.

Research Journal and Sketchbook Exercise 4

1. Who is the best storyteller you know? Write about this person and why you have designated them the best story-teller you know. Now write a letter to them, including an explanation for why you see them as the best storyteller you know.
2. Draw a chronological life line highlighting the major events/experiences in your life from birth to present. Then write at least three pages describing your chronological timeline.
3. Find a photograph of yourself. Write at least three pages sharing everything you can think of related to that photo. Then write at least three pages of a fictional account of the photo. How were these two writing exercises different? The same?
4. Interview someone for 20–30 minutes asking them to tell you about their life and then write at least three pages sharing what you learned. Within your writing, sketch a visual representation of the experience.
5. Ask a writing partner to co-write with you on a shared document, such as a Google Doc, about a person you both know something about. It can be a real person or a fictional character. The co-writing must result in a single-authored essay (you will jointly decide what your pen name will be). Reflect on how you created this essay and what and how you negotiated the creation.

These types of writing exercises can bring you closer to the working questions life writers encounter. What did these five writing exercises reveal to you?

Chapter 2 will introduce ideas that guide life writers' method-ological approaches.

References

Abbott, H. P. (2008). *The Cambridge Introduction to Narrative*. Cambridge: Cambridge University Press.

Baena, R. (2013). *Transculturing Auto/biography: Forms of Life Writing*. London: Routledge.

Bakhtin, M. (1986). *Speech Genres and Other Late Essays*. Trans. Vern W. McGee. Austin: University of Texas Press.

Bakhtin, M. (1992). *The Dialogic Imagination: Four Essays*. Austin: University of Texas Press.

Cannella, G. S., & Lincoln, Y. S. (2012). Deploying qualitative methods for critical social purposes. In S. R. Steinberg & G. S. Cannella (Eds.), *Critical Qualitative Research Reader* (pp. 104–113). New York: Peter Lang.

Couser, T. (2005). Genre matters: Form, force, and filiation. *Life Writing, 1*, 139–156.

Couser, T. (2009). *Signifying Bodies: Disability in Contemporary Life Writing*. Corporealities: Discourses of Disability. Ann Arbor: University of Michigan Press.

Crenshaw, K. (1989). *Demarginalizing the Intersection of Race and Sex: A Black Feminist Critique of Antidiscrimination Doctrine, Feminist Theory and Antiracist Politics*. University of Chicago Legal Forum, pp. 139–168.

Creswell, J. (2013). *Qualitative Inquiry and Research Design: Choosing Among Five Approaches* (3rd ed.). Thousand Oaks, CA: Sage.

Davies, W. (2014). Neoliberalism: A bibliographic review. *Theory Culture and Society, 31*(7–8), 309–317.

Davis, L. (1995). *Enforcing Normalcy: Disability, Deafness, and the Body*. New York: Norton.

Denzin, N. K. (2010). Pedagogical practices: Teaching qualitative research. In *Qualitative Manifesto: A Call to Arms* (pp. 51–70). Walnut Creek, CA: Left Coast Press.

Denzin, N. K., & Giardina, M. D., Eds. (2013). *Global Dimensions of Qualitative Inquiry* (Vol. 8). Walnut Creek, CA: Left Coast Press.

Denzin, N. K. (1989/2014). *Interpretive Biography*. Newbury Park, CA: Sage.

Egan, S., & Helms, G. (2002). Auto/biography? Yes. But Canadian?. Retrieved from http://canlit.ca/canlitmedia/pdfs/articles/canlit172-Autobiography(EganHelms).pdf

Eisner, E. (1991). *The Enlightened Eye: Qualitative Inquiry and the Enhancement of Educational Practice*. New York: Macmillan.

Ferri, B. (October, 2011). Disability life writing and the politics of knowing. *Teachers College Record, 113*(10), 2267–2282.

Flick, U. (2014). *An Introduction to Qualitative Research* (5th ed.). Thousand Oaks, CA: Sage.

Freire, P. (1970). *Pedagogy of the Oppressed*. Trans. Myra Bergman Ramos. New York: Continuum.

Gilmore, L. (2001). *The Limits of Autobiography: Trauma and Testimony*. Ithaca: Cornell University Press.

Heilbrun, C. G. (1988). *Writing a Woman's Life*. New York: W.W. Norton & Co.

Kadar, M. (1992). *Essays on Life Writing: From Genre to Critical Practice* (Vol. 11). Toronto, Canada: University of Toronto Press.

Kadar, M. (2014). Coming to terms: Life writing – From genre to critical practice. In H. Renders & B. De Haan (Eds.), *Theoretical Discussions of Biography* (pp. 195–205). Boston: Brill.

Kelly, D. (2013). Africa, North. In M. Jolly (Ed.), *Encyclopedia of Life Writing: Autobiographical and Biographical Forms* (pp. 7–9). London: Routledge.

Kridel, C., Ed. (1998). *Writing Educational Biography*. New York: Garland/Routledge.

Lakoff, G., & Johnson, M. (2003/1980). *Metaphors We Live By*. Chicago: University of Chicago Press.

Leavy, P. (2013). *Fiction as Research Practice: Short Stories, Novellas, and Novels* (Vol. 11). Walnut Creek: Left Coast Press.

Leavy, P. (2016). *American Circumstance* (Anniversary ed.). Rotterdam/Boston/Taipei: Sense Publishers.

McChesney (1999). Introduction. In N. Chomsky (Ed.). *Profit over People: Neoliberalism and Global Order* (pp. 7–16). New York: Seven Stories Press.

Mills, C. W. (1959). *The Sociological Imagination*. Oxford: Oxford University Press.

Mitchell, D., & Snyder, S. (2000). *Narrative Prosthesis: Disability and the Dependencies of Discourse*. Ann Arbor: University of Michigan Press.

Mollow, A. (2002). "When black women start going on Prozac . . ." The politics of race, gender, and emotional distress in Meri Nana-Ama Danquah's *Willow Weep for Me*. In L. Davis (Ed.), *The Disability Studies Reader* (2nd ed., pp. 265–283). New York: Routledge.

Moore-Gilbert, B. (2009). *Postcolonial Life-Writing: Culture, Politics and Self-Representation*. New York: Routledge.

Mulvihill, T. (2000). Sarton may I? Using the life and work of May Sarton as a pedagogical tool. *Vitae Scholasticae: The Bulletin of Educational Biography*, *18*(2) [Fall 1999 (Caddo Gap Press, arrived in print Spring, 2000)], 95–106.

Pasque, P., Carducci, R., Kuntz, A. K., & Gildersleeve, R. E. (2012). *Qualitative Inquiry for Equity in Higher Education: Methodological Implications, Negotiations and Responsibilities* [ASHE Higher Education Report, 37(6)]. San Francisco, CA: Jossey-Bass.

Peterson, L. H. (1986). *Victorian Autobiography: The Tradition of Self-Interpretation*. New Haven: Yale University Press.

Ricoeur, P. (2010). *Time and Narrative* (Vol. 3). Chicago: University of Chicago Press.

Sherry, M. (2005). Reading me/me reading disability. *Prose Studies*, *27*(1–2), 163–175.

Singh, S. R. (2016). Life-writing and the Disabled Self: Discourses on Subjectivity. Retrieved from www.inter-disciplinary.net/probing-the-boundaries/wp-content/uploads/2016/02/Sandeep-R.-Singh-Draft-Paper.pdf.

Smith, L. M. (1994). Biographical method. In N. Denzin & Y. S. Lincoln (Eds.), *Handbook of Qualitative Research* (pp. 286-305). Thousand Oaks, CA: Sage.

Smith, L. M. (2012). Nora Barlow: A tale of a Darwin granddaughter. *Vitae Scholasticae*, *29*(2), 58–76.

Smith, L. M. (2014). Adventuring as biographers: A chronicle of a difficult ten-day week. *Vitae Scholasticae*, *31*(1), 5–22.

Solorzano, D. G. & Yosso, T. J. (2002). Critical race methodology: Counter-storytelling as an analytical framework for education research. *Qualitative Inquiry*, *8*(1), 23–44.

Spivak, G. C. (1988). Can the subaltern speak? an idea. In P. Williams & L. Chrisman (Eds.), *Colonial Discourse and Postcolonial Theory* (pp. 21–78). New York: Columbia University Press.

Swaminathan, R., & Mulvihill, T. (2017). *Critical Questions for Qualitative Research*. New York: Routledge.

Zucker, M. S. (2015). Memory to ink: Autobiography project in Portugal. *European Journal of Life Writing*, *4*, 1–12.

2

THEORIES AND APPROACHES THAT GUIDE CRITICAL LIFE WRITERS

In this chapter, we examine the different ways in which critical life writing projects have been approached and the methodological questions that arise within these projects when different modes of inquiry are used. For example, the analytic tools suggested by Kridel's (1998) guiding principles for constructing educational biography are different from Stephen Oates's description of three approaches to biography: the scholarly chronicle, the critical study, and the narrative biography (Oates, 1986; 1991). We provide researchers with tools to carry out life writing projects by suggesting ways to conduct a project from start to finish. This includes choosing a topic or subject, examining lives as living data, understanding the role of documents and artifacts, learning to tell the story, and finally writing/performing/displaying through the voice of the life writer.

Biography

There has been a long and illustrious history describing the various approaches biographers have taken when trying to convey the fullness and the particulars of an individual life. Historians and literary writers have most often been the life writers associated with the genre referred to as biography. In fact, Virginia Woolf's famous quote, "My God, how does one write a Biography?" is still an often-repeated one by all who venture into this form of life writing. In this book we pick up the story about biography with what qualitative researchers have referred to as the narrative turn or the biographical turn in our qualitative inquiry projects and argue that Woolf's question is a living, breathing question that ought not be presumed answerable in definitive terms, yet that provokes a continuously open inquiry guiding biographical projects and, in fact, all life writing projects. Weaving together parts of what we know collectively about biography writing from literary biographers, historical biographers, social science biographers, etc. can help set the stage for preparing qualitative researchers and social science writers for life writing.

C. Wright Mills, for example, provides us a clear and actionable space when he says "no social study that does not come back to the problems of biography, of history and of their intersections within a society has completed its intellectual journey" (C. Wright Mills, 1959, p. 6). He remains a touchstone for all social scientists grappling with what he so poetically referred to as "the sociological imagination," imploring us to stay cognizant of how the human imagination is both impacted by the lived experience, as theorized by sociological concepts, while serving as a forward-shaping force for ways to construct a meaningful life. In line with his thinking, biographers have high interest in the contours of a life and often enjoy the process of assembling artifacts, letters (or epistolary collections), journals, diaries, photographs, works of art, and other materials that help evoke or provoke a telling of a life. Such tellings of lives draw connections between individual life stories and wider frameworks of understanding: between individuals and culture, or individuals and society. The ontological assumption in the "biographical turn" is that individuals have agency. Biography, like other forms of life writing, assumes that individuals make a difference and can have an effect on society.

Historical Tracings of the Approach

As stories evolve and are culturally, socially, and historically constructed in relation to notions of self, the tools and approaches that qualitative researchers use to create their narratives also change and evolve. Historians cite the fourth century BCE as the time when the Greek term "bios" emerged that distinguished biography as a genre of writing distinct from history. Early biographical writings described character traits and their influences on leadership and served to provide role models for readers to emulate or as warnings of what brought about failure. For example, Plutarch's depiction of Mark Antony was an analysis of the ways in which Mark Antony's private life and passions led him to fail as a Roman leader. During the Middle Ages in Europe, hagiographies of saints began to appear. Examples of such hagiographies in Europe included Bede's St. Cuthbert in the eighth century and Eadmer's Anselm in the twelfth century. In India the Jain monk Hemachandra wrote *Lives* of sixty-three illustrious persons or heroes. In hagiographies, the character of the subject is depicted as "saintly." Biographies that are similar to hagiographies written today are most often commemorative biographies of historical figures. A new model for biographical writing that moved away from hagiography to a more realistic portrayal of lives was introduced by Samuel Johnson and James Boswell in the eighteenth century. They provided a new model for biographical writing that focused on the lives of ordinary people and what they did in their everyday lives. Johnson believed that every human being possessed negative traits and that a convincing biography would contain both—the positive and the negative.

Despite Johnson's and Boswell's model, biographers continued to avoid writing details of lives that might veer on the disreputable. Carlyle critiqued the "Damocles sword of respectability" that prevented biographers from writing about issues that might prove disturbing. Biographers who took up the challenge of writing in the new model were not spared criticism. Elizabeth Gaskell is a case in point, whose *Life of Charlotte Bronte* (1857) was criticized as being too explicit and revealing and drew the ire of the public. After World War I, biographical writing changed with the advent of Freudian psychology and an anti-Victorian sentiment. It was Lytton Strachey's *Eminent Victorians* published in 1918 that brought to light new types of biography writing. Strachey explained that biographers needed to be artists and that the portraits they drew of their subjects needed to be drawn from all available material to expose the less complimentary angles of their subjects along with their positive features. However, such biographies were also criticized for "muck raking" while psychobiographies shaped by Freud's work were regarded as too simplistic for focusing on the subjects' motivations. It was Virginia Woolf (1939), who questioned the metaphor of biographer as artist and argued that the biographer was as much a craftsman as an artist, drawing on both the skills of a craftsman in that biographers are constrained by the conditions of biography that needed to be grounded in facts and, on the other hand, needing the imagination of an artist to reveal the inner workings of the subject's mind. She declared that biography was neither art nor craft but something "betwixt and between." Critical approaches to biographical life writing is similarly neither hagiographic nor purely imaginative, and tries to depict a subject's multi-dimensional life that reveals the conflicts, the questions and uncovers a deeper layer of meaning. In biography, as with other forms of life writing, several questions guide the topic, problem, or main interest. Perhaps the most important question for biographers is to ask the questions: Will this biography reveal a greater understanding of this person's life? And will a narrative of their everyday life reveal or open up an understanding of the complexity and multiplicity of human experience?

Sub-fields within biography have grown, and we present a few here that a qualitative researcher who wishes to write a dissertation or embark on a new project might find useful. We picked archival projects as an enduring method for writing within this genre, collective biographies as a new and exciting development within life writing, and educational biography as an exemplar of a genre that combines several methods that biographers can use in any discipline. These sub-fields of biography have grown to include many forms, some of which we describe in this chapter. Archival biographies, collective biographies, and educational biographies, in particular, are forms that might be most useful for students of life writing to undertake biographical projects.

Archival Biographical Projects

Archival biographical projects are somewhat like an adventure where we have a general sense of the territory or perhaps the starting point, but we need to create the map ourselves. Before we begin to think about what we can do in the archives, we need to have an idea of what we can find in archives, where to go for particular materials, and how to start. In archives, we can find not only materials pertaining to famous people, but the life writings of ordinary people. Letters, diaries, family writings, cookbooks, photographs, autobiographies are all exemplars of the types of material that can be found in archives. The tradition of archiving such material started at the beginning of the twentieth century in North America and Europe.

Life writers often engage with archived materials such as: sketchbooks; photographs; videos; journals and diaries; newspaper clippings; letters and emails; tweets, blogs, and other social media posts; reports; scripts from radio, television, and theatrical productions; institutional history records; maps; books (published and unpublished); and lists. These documents represent the types of materials life writers use to conduct a document analysis otherwise known as "a systematic procedure for reviewing or evaluation documents—both printed and electronic [and they] contain text (words) and images that have been recorded without a researcher's intervention" (Bowen, 2009, p. 27). Archival documents can be found in public as well as private archives, at University libraries, and research centers. The former are prepared for an audience while with the latter it is not necessarily the case.

Archives can often be regarded, misleadingly, as neutral sites of primary research materials. However, it is important for the archival life writer to be aware that collections are the result of social hierarchies and assumptions regarding whose lives are worth recording, documenting, and preserving. Archives are the result of decisions, political and social, that regulate what could and should be collected. As Tesar (2015) has pointed out, archives have an "air of calmness" that can be misleading. Archival research is as subject to questions of ethical responsibility as life writing methods that utilize "human subject approvals." Although ethics committees may not seek an IRB for archival research, it is nevertheless true that archival research can raise up questions of ethics.

Life writers who approach archives from a critical approach need to be mindful of the power of archives. "Gatekeepers" exist in archival research as much as in other forms of life writing. In archives, they are individuals who guard the archival material and its access and wield power in terms of what knowledge gains visibility and to what extent and at what point in time. Tesar (2015) tells the story of archival research in several institutions, public and private, and how much or little access was allowed depending on the gatekeepers. At some places, the difficulty of access was compounded by the lack of organization of primary source data, while at others, the gatekeepers decided when the research must stop and denied access thereafter.

Life writers, as archival researchers, need to be equipped and prepared to work in the archives as much as they would need to prepare to hone their interview skills if they chose life history as their approach of choice. Connors (1992) suggested that archival researchers should start with a hypothesis and then go into the archives and "play." His suggestion can be interpreted to mean that life writers need to keep an open mind and be ready to encounter the hoped for unexpected or the serendipitous find. However, scholars who have worked in archives and have suffered from "archive fever" suggest that it is important for researchers to know what they are looking for and when to exit the archive. Archive fever is tantamount to feeling lost in the labyrinths of boxes and files and digital repositories and, worse, feeling a sense of helplessness or of being overwhelmed at the responsibility of decoding and interpreting and doing justice to the vast material one confronts. Our suggestions for life writers who want to work in archives are to go the route of systematic research with an eye open for the creative possibility.

To this end, we offer some suggestions for life writers conducting archival research:

1. The topic or "life" one is interested in serves as the primary guide. Reading secondary sources can give a researcher a sense of what is known and what questions the researcher may want to ask.
2. Determine what data are available. A web search can yield rich results. Internet searches for archival materials on a given topic or on a person entails searching in the "deep web." The "deep web" is that part of the internet which is not necessarily easily searched through ordinary search terms in the search engines one uses every day. These search engines such as Google or Yahoo are a good first step but cannot get at the "deep web." Searching

the "deep web" means locating directories of archival repositories, obtaining websites of archival organizations, finding online bibliographies, searching finding aids that have short descriptions of materials in archives, and searching digitized primary sources. The WorldCat registry is a good place to start to find archival repositories. There are data archives across the world that contain vast amounts of data on many different subjects.

3. Data might be publicly available or in private collections. Determine where the data are available. Email or call archives and tell them briefly about the topic of your research. Ask them for materials you might already know are available and ask for further suggestions.

4. Ask archivists what you are allowed to bring into the archives for working. For example, some archives may allow you to take photographs of documents, and others might allow a document scanner to be brought in. A small portable document scanner might be a worthwhile investment if you have vast amounts of data to examine within a limited amount of time.

5. Some archives are digitally available. Ask what materials need special permissions or consent of living relatives or estate representatives and contact them via letter, email or phone for consent. Be sure to include an outline of your project and why you think it would be valuable to view the materials.

6. Think through the timeline and budget costs of your research and factor in travel and scanning, photocopying, or document photograph costs.

The analysis of materials gathered in the archives can be approached in a number of ways. The most frequently used method is one of content analysis. At first, the researcher reads materials in the archives and catalogues or categorizes it in some way. Next, reading and taking notes in relation to the research questions can narrow down the focus of what is considered important or not. If we were researching narratives of new teachers, for example, their journals would be as important to read as their lesson plans. For the researcher, reading is the first act of interpretation and the notes one takes while reading form the first act of analysis. These could fall under the realm of "interesting quotes," or be organized chronologically, or be organized according to themes in terms of the work that was done by the person who is being researched. There are many different ways to organize what one reads. Analysis of content is much like most analyses of qualitative data and involves several steps. Wolcott (2009) refers to these steps as description, analysis, and then interpretation, or the DAI method, and Fairclough (2001) explains the same processes as description, interpretation, and explanation.

The most important steps in analyzing archival data involve the following:

1. Select data that are related to your research questions;
2. Think through criteria for inclusion or exclusion of data;
3. Create coding protocols—determine how to categorize the data into segments and label each segment with a code;
4. Create thematic protocols—determine criteria regarding codes that should be grouped into themes (which codes go with which themes);
5. Draw a table with all the codes, criteria for each code, and criteria for each theme—this will become your coding companion.

In the coding companion, make adjustments continuously as data are being analyzed to either create new sets of codes or themes or to merge some codes under existing themes.

Archives often contain image-based data. While it is not our intention here to give an in-depth explanation of how to analyze image or visual data, we urge life writers to examine photographs and other visual data such as scrapbooks and drawings and to treat them with the same analytical lens and rigorous questioning. Photographs and image data are often most likely to be under-catalogued and found only through browsing files. There are repositories of image data that researchers can view; for example, ArtSTOR is a digital library of nearly one million images from several disciplines. When examining visual data, the context of image creation needs to be a focus for the researcher—who created the images, for whom, and for what purpose are all critical questions for the researcher to keep in mind. In other words, the circumstances in which the images are created are as important to the research as the image itself.

Research Journal and Sketchbook Exercise 5

Choose a photograph that intrigues you. It can be a portrait or a picture with a collection of people preferably doing an activity of some kind.

1. Write a few words that come to your mind when you see the picture.
2. Put away the picture and try to recollect the picture in words as best as you can. Then take your sketchbook and draw the picture or a representation of the picture as best as you can.
3. Look at the picture again. Now write a caption for the picture.
4. Briefly describe the picture in your own words and identify or underline your own assumptions.
5. Try to read related textual sources and see what facts can be uncovered about the photograph or image.
6. Write a paragraph reflecting on the process of analyzing this image and the assumptions you made and how they were modified with more information.

Archives often contain the official documentation of events with little from the perspective of those whose lives were impacted by policies. In order to access the voices of the marginalized, and those whose voices are barely present in official records, scholars have taken to oral history as a corrective methodology. Later we elaborate on oral history methods and outline the different ways in which stories from archives can be retold. In the next section we describe collective biography as an innovative methodology that has emerged from feminists' work that at times interweaves notions of memory, embodiment, and subjectivity.

Collective Biography

Collective biography is an innovative method of life writing, originating in feminist research in the work of Haug (1987) and developing and growing over time. Although there have been attempts to articulate rules of collective biographical method, Gonick, Walsh, and Brown (2011) point out that the practice of collective biography has no firm rules, thereby lending credence to a multiplicity of approaches. Some scholars stressed that "the very heterogeneity of everyday life demands similarly heterogeneous methods if it is to be understood" (Haug et al., 1987, pp. 70–71). It is not surprising therefore to find that researchers have approached collective biography in different ways. For some researchers, the data for collective biography is generated by the researcher(s) themselves as they form their own research team bound by self-announced sociological or identity commonalities. The memory work they engage in collectively helps produce the written data they jointly arrange and analyze. According to Hawkins, Al-Hindi, Moss, and Kern:

> As a feminist approach to research, collective biography draws centrally on the idea that significant memories are critical in the constitution of the self, and maintains that in analyzing memories collectively, researchers can begin to tap into wider social processes and structures.
>
> (2016, p. 165)

For others, it is writing biographies of a group of people who are connected in some way. For example, Berta Morgan's dissertation focused on the founding members of the American Association of University Women (AAUW). In the case of this archival study there were differing amounts of archival data available for each woman, yet when pulled together collectively she was able to generate a biography about this group of women that had never been attempted before (see Morgan, 2013). Still others look upon collective biography as a way of researching a group of individuals who share a particular area, activity, or field so that there is deeper understanding of the individual lives as well as the field or activity (Weiner, 2008). An example is Jane Martin's (2005) use of the term "collective biography" to describe her work on the social networks of women activists in London during the late nineteenth and early twentieth centuries. And the work of another group of researchers looking at the concept and experience of joy within academic labor (Kern, Hawkins, Al-Hindi, and Moss, 2014) is another example.

Collective biography can be used in many fields. For example, let's look at how geographers are employing this approach. Feminist geographers have engaged

> a rich toolkit of approaches, including interviews, focus groups, participant observation, and life writing. All of these approaches investigate human experience, entail reflexivity on the part of the researcher, and attempt to connect individual experiences to social structures. All raise epistemological questions about the relationships among perception, experience, truth, and representation.
>
> (Hawkins et al., 2016, p. 167)

Collective biography, as a form of life writing, may entail collaborative work similar to some other forms of qualitative research and life writing. Davies, for example, has used collective biography methods with small groups of people who make decisions together on the research questions and design a set of protocols and questions that can serve to fuel memory work (Davies, 2006). Each participant writes up several memories based on the agreed-upon research question. Multiple drafts are produced with the help of questions from each participant/researcher with a view to refining the writing so that the sensations in the body produced by the memory are illustrated and described as accurately as possible. In addition, the process of the construction of the subject made equally as transparent as the structures of society, institutions, and relationships of power that shape the "self" are all described and then collectively analyzed. The goal of such collective biographical writing is that of empowerment and emancipation. This use of collective biography has much in common with critical, feminist approaches to life writing as well as versions of collaborative autoethnography. In keeping with Haug's (1987, p. 70) point that "no single 'true' method . . . is alone appropriate to this kind of work," we find that scholars have continued to experiment and push the methodological boundaries of autoethnography, collaborative autoethnography, autobiography, and collective biography in ways that move away from the idea of a singular or correct mode of life writing. Scholars of feminist geography have attempted to explain the blurred boundaries and the attempts at distinctions between autobiography, autoethnography, and collective biography. Autobiography and autoethnography are the most used forms of life writing among feminist geographers. While autobiography focuses on an individual life and particular themes within that life (Smith and Watson, 2010), autoethnography involves the telling of the contextual story that includes the lives of a group of whom the author is a member (Ellis, 2004). Collective biography brings together the possibility of focusing on the individual life as well as the structure that produces the biographical self. However, as we have earlier pointed out, the three forms of life writing have much in common, a point reiterated by Hawkins et al. (2016). The three features that autobiography, autoethnography, and collective biography share are "an iterative quality in the writing of the texts, a critical reflexivity sensitive to power relations, and an affinity with analyzing processes of subject formation" (p. 167). In our experience of these forms of life writing, we confirm that these three features are crucial and present. The practice of iterative writing invokes a reflexivity that asks questions of the context and the individual incident or narrative as well as the narrator's stance. The resulting reflective writing produces a narrative that is closer to depicting the immediacy of experiences. In addition to the iterative process, life writers need to be aware of relationships of power that are present in research situations. In autobiography, the researcher in recounting stories of the self will inevitably also discuss context and other participants with whom the research has contact and relationships. The life writer of autobiography needs to be mindful of power relations in two ways—first, in depicting the story of the singular self in relation to others, the researcher needs to ask, how do these inadvertent participants figure in the story and what power do they have to respond to the text? In the second instance, the power of the narrator is shared with the readers, as they can interpret and make judgments on the choices and ethics of the autobiographer's life, a point made early on by Michel Leiris (1946) when he described the autobiographer as a bullfighter, who makes himself vulnerable to the reader as the bullfighter does to the horn of the bull. Since then, scholars have referred to the interplay between the text and the reader, the narrator and the subject (Long, 1992), and have reflected on the complex web of all four in life writing projects.

Critical reflection in the process of analysis is the third feature that draws these forms of life writing together. The iterative process and reflexivity both come into play in the analytical process, "a process that layers multiple positionings and individual histories of a group of selves into the written memories" (Hawkins et al., 2016, p. 170). In the analysis and subsequent narrative, life writers in auto-ethnography, autobiography, and collective biography look for the processes of subject formation. Questions of truth become complicated as the narrative and the memory or the experience are both examined for the truth they contain. This is a particular feature of life writing genres as distinct from other qualitative research where the verification of data might be considered differently by considering trustworthiness or thick description (Geertz, 1994; Creswell, 2013). Truth in life writing is found through resonance (Hawkins et al., 2016). In life writing, one must find ways to deal with those preoccupied with the dilemmas of truth-telling (Stanley, 1993; Ellis, 2004; Davies and Gannon, 2006b).

Scholars of collective biography point out that the life writing form values the memories of small incidents usually written off or considered marginal and brings those memories to life through invoking the sensations of the body. Virginia Woolf (1985) invokes sensations of the body similarly in *Moments of Being* when she says, "I was hardly aware of myself, only of the sensation" (p. 66). Collective biographers emphasize sensations as an aid to memory and urge researchers to take the ordinary, the everyday experience, seriously and to interrogate it for power, structures of relations. Collective biography introduces and uses the experiences of the body as a way to nudge and examine memories through the body—the smells, the feelings, the emotions. As collective biographers assert, "sensations of pressure and pulling on muscles and joints, as well as feelings in a throat, stomach, or shoulders may anchor recollections" (Hawkins et al., 2016, p. 173).

Hawkins et al. have developed what they refer to as the nine *Hallmarks of Collective Biography*:

1. Researcher experiences are the sole sources of data
2. Collectivity is critical in data collection and analysis
3. Extensive and even participation of researchers must occur at all stages of research
4. Critical reflection is integrated into each step of the research process
5. Data collection and analysis are both iterative
6. Subjectivity and subject formation are central theoretical interests in analysis
7. Embodiment is foregrounded in data collection
8. Emotions and affect can be readily accessed through data collection
9. Spatial processes and place specificity are both foregrounded and readily accessed through data collection.

(Hawkins et al., 2016, p. 169)

While all elements of their collective biography hallmarks are worthy of consideration, let's look more closely at Hallmark 9 and the creative practice of fieldnotes and analytic memos prepared as diagrams and drawn or arranged as "tea sandwiches" (triangular shapes) and "paninis" (square shapes), where they served as guides for data analysis (Hawkins et al., 2016, p. 170). Their use of diagrams in these shapes allows them to recollect and record not only memories that are infused with and nudged by sensations of the body but also memories that are spatial and place specific. Hawkins et al. (2016) add a spatial dimension to memory work in collective biography. In their words:

> These spatialities are important in understanding how bodies, subjects, and experiences form (Kern et al., 2014; see also Longhurst, 2005), particularly in light of what surfaces as mattering in analyzing our own memories.

(p. 174)

Hawkins et al. ascribe to a version of collective biography that is a close cousin to duoethnography and forms of autoethnography referred to as "collective autoethnography" or "collaborative autoethnography." Collective biographies are at times also called "group biographies" (Peters, 1981), where the researcher weaves a narrative of several lives and their interconnections. Yet, there are other forms of collective biography that life writers use, such as prosopography, a term used to describe a biographical approach when examining a group whose individual biographies are too partial or largely incomplete, yet when pieced together form a collective narrative about the group. For example, Samantha-Jayne Oldfield (2015) published an article within the field of sport history where she argues for the distinctions between biography, collective biography, and prosopography. She explains that biographies are constructed with "key information . . . the what, why, where, when, who, how, and why dimensions are the backbone of the narrative" (Oldfield, 2015, p. 1861). A prosopographical approach to biography can analyze individual biographies thematically and as a group. This approach is useful to better understand the patterns and relationships of groups. For a prosopographical analysis, the group examined must have enough in common for relationships and patterns to be uncovered. An example of a prosopographical analysis is Josie Abbot's (2009) study of women office secretarial workers in the late nineteenth and early twentieth centuries. Prosopography therefore describes "'external features of a population that the researcher has determined has something in common', following the interrogation of biographical information" (Oldfield, 2015, p. 1864). Oldfield points to Poulsen's collective biography using archival data sources focusing on physical education teachers (1900–1940) as the "first modern prosopography in sport history" (Oldfield, 2015, p. 1868).

Some scholars have conflated collective biography with prosopography, using the terms similarly, while other scholars such as Magdalino (2003) and Oldfield (2015) have strived to make a distinction between the two. The main distinction is that collective biographies value the individual biographies as they are shaped together for the biography of the group, while in prosopography, the focus is more on the collective and less on the individual biographies making up the group. Magdalino suggests that prosopography is useful in places where the records are sparse and therefore more difficult to craft into a biographical narrative. The goal is to collect data that transcend individual lives and tell us more about social mobility or status or stratification.

As Oldfield further explains, it is a focus primarily on the aggregate of individuals (Oldfield, p. 1865).

An example of a recent study using prosopography is Jenkinson's (1993; 2016) study of one hundred Scottish medical practitioners who were also shopkeepers in the late nineteenth and early twentieth centuries. Her work drew connections between medicine and pharmacy as her investigation into the careers and education of the "marginal men" through court cases; census data found that a significant number of them had experience as chemists prior to becoming medical practitioners. A second example of a prosopography is one based on semi-structured interviews of French Olympians between 1945 and 1972, which is authored by Erard and Bancel (2007).

Educational Biography

Educational biography is a form of life writing that focuses on the biographies of educators, the educative storylines of any individual or group, or the various innovative pedagogies that make use of life writing. Educational biography, as a term, has been most associated with the *International Society for Educational Biography* (ISEB) founded in 1982 and comprised of an interdisciplinary group of social scientists creating and experimenting with various forms of life writing. This group has continuously published a journal, *Vitae Scholasticae*, and hosted an annual conference. The term "educational biography" was also elevated by the edited collection curated by Craig Kridel, *Writing Educational Biography: Explorations in Qualitative Research* (1998), as he led the way in helping scholars contemplate the methodologies and the affiliated methods life writers were developing and applying to their projects related to educational biography. Many examples of the various forms and types of educational biography can be found in *Vitae Scholasticae*, the only refereed journal dedicated solely to such projects. For example see the following:

Kelly, H. (2013). Toward a critical race biography of Marion Thompson Wright (1905–1962): Finding facts, pivoting race. *Vitae Schloasticae: The Journal of Educational Biography, 30*(2), 43–65.

Leggo, C. (2005). Autobiography and identity: Six speculations. *Vitae Scholasticae: The Journal of Educational Biography, 22*(1), 115–133.

Leggo, C. (2005). Autobiography and identity: Six speculations. *Vitae Scholasticae: The Journal of Educational Biography, 22*(1), 115–133.

Leggo, C. (2004). Light and shadow: Four reasons for writing (and not writing) autobiographically. *Vitae Scholasticae: The Journal of Educational Biography, 21*(1), 5–22.

Mulvihill, T. (2000). Sarton May I? Using the life and work of May Sarton as a pedagogical tool. *Vitae Scholasticae: The Bulletin of Educational Biography, 18*(2) [Fall 1999 (Caddo Gap Press, arrived in-print Spring, 2000)], 95–106.

Smith, L. M. (2012). Nora Barlow: A tale of a Darwin granddaughter. *Vitae Scholasticae, 29*(2).

Smith, L. M. (2014). Adventuring as biographers: A chronicle of a difficult ten-day week. *Vitae Scholasticae,* 31(1), 5–22.

Educational biography can also be found in books that provide insights into this type of life writing. For example, see Louis M. Smith (2000), *A Perspective on Biography: Domain, Variety, and Complexity*, where he contends that biographers must remain cognizant of their process and be as methodologically descript as possible. Also see Craig Kridel (1998), *Writing Educational Biography*, a collection of chapters that helped map the growing field in the late 1990s.

And under the category of comparative educational biography, you can find the following examples:

Clifford, G. J. (1989). *Lone Voyagers: Academic Women in Coeducational Universities, 1870–1937.* New York: Feminist Press at the City University of New York.

Clifford, G. J. (2014). *Those Good Gertrudes: A Social History of Women Teachers in America.* Baltimore, MD: Johns Hopkins University Press.

Mulvihill, T. (1999). Hart to Hart: Sisters working in tandem for educational change in nineteenth century America. *Vitae Scholasticae: The Bulletin of Educational Biography, 18*(1), 79–95.

Mulvihill, T. (Autumn, 2009) The universal declaration of human rights and education: Examining the issues and vital voices for women and girls through comparative educational biography. *Hudson Valley Review, 26*(1), 53–67.

Urban, W. J. (2012). *Leaders in the Historical Study of American Education* (Vol. 3). New York: Springer Science & Business Media.

One of the processes of data collection in educational biography, or in any form of biography when selecting a living subject, is the interview. Several types of interviews are utilized for different life writing projects and biography is no exception. An example of an interview method for biographical life writing that is advocated by Szczepanik and Siebert (2015) in their research into the lives of prisoners is Schutze's (1983) method of the biographical interview. They draw a distinction between the traditional interview and the biographical interview method of Schutze (1983). One of the features of the biographical interview is the role of the researcher being in the background and that of the narrator being foregrounded. In Schutze's (1983) method, the interviewee is referred to as the narrator as a way to centralize the importance of the narrator and to emphasize that the interview itself is a narration rather than a question-and-answer list. The researcher in this type of interview does not direct the interview in any way and instead waits for the narrator to lead the way. It is at the end of the narrative that the interviewer asks questions of clarification or any other questions relating to the objectives of the research. Szczepanik and Siebert (2015) in their prison research explain that they were able to obtain rich narratives from the narrators or participants because of the "triple bind of narration" that is a unique feature of how Schutze (1983) explains his biographical method. The triple bind of narration is the pressure that narrators face while recounting their life stories to close the narrative, to condense the stories, and at the same time provide sufficient detail. The requirement to condense pressures the narrators to talk about what they consider critical since they cannot tell the whole story, the requirement to close induces them to make meaning and reflect on particular events or people in their lives, and the requirement to provide detail means they narrate the contexts within which some events took place. In their research on prisons, Szczepanik and Siebert (2015) found that the strength of the method lay in the triple bind of narrative and in the reflexivity that this generated, resulting in biographical narratives that employed a range of interpretive categories as opposed to the typical biographies told for the benefit of parole boards. These narratives allowed for a deeper understanding into the world of prisons and prisoners.

Edel (1984) described four dilemmas that all biographers must confront in the process of research analysis. First is the dilemma of separation of the biographer and the subject. A second is the dilemma of data reduction. A third is the dilemma of analysis and researching simultaneously and a fourth is the dilemma of writing it all up. Biographers have to acknowledge that they are always outside of the minds of their subjects, even as they seek to understand and glean insights from the experiences of the subject. To extend this further, we can say that one can never know "completely" all that there is to know about the participant, and the biographer would have to contend with the idea of partial stories or incompleteness. Data analysis concerns of researchers often center on how to manage to "reduce" the vast collection of stories, letters, documents, and other data to a size and form that can then be organized into the life and story that the biographer wants to tell. This problem is related to the issue of figuring out how to create an order, pattern, or logic out of various documents that represent the complexity of a flowing, dynamic, complex life. How can one reduce a life to a pattern and yet tell the story of life? Another problem concerns the positionality of the biographer. How can the biographer remain immersed in the life of the subject and yet stand outside of it enough to analyze the experiences? Edel's (1984) solution to these dilemmas was through psychoanalytic theory and by the biographer becoming an artist in order to meet the demands of interpretation and narration. An awareness of one's own positionality would allow the biographer to walk the tightrope of being close enough to the subject to be empathetic and understanding while at the same time far enough to not be subsumed by the identity of the subject or become so close that analysis would become difficult. In qualitative research, this dilemma has often been referred to and couched in cautionary terms as researchers have been reminded of the dangers of "going native" or adopting the worldview of the participant to the extent that the researcher is no longer standing on the outside. We, the authors of this book, urge biographers and qualitative researchers to stand at those borderlands that we believe to be permeable so as to traverse those spaces between the inner landscape of the participants' experiences and those of the researcher's own experiences. It is in the dialogue between those images that we believe a story emerges that is both the story of the biographical subject and that of the researcher.

Joyce Antler's (1989) *Lucy Sprague Mitchell: The Making of a Modern Woman* is a groundbreaking educational biography about the founder of Bank Street College of Education who was also the first dean of women at the University of California, Berkeley. Sara Lawrence Lightfoot's (1988) *Balm in Gilead: Journey of a Healer* conveys the educational biography of several generations of an African American family researched and written from the perspective of a daughter who is a notable university faculty member, sociologist, and qualitative research methodologist (i.e., known for portraiture).

Challenges

Life writers today continue to debate these issues and wrestle with challenges in the arenas of how to conceptualize or think about the process of constructing biographies, issues surrounding the "truth-value" of a person's life or how to determine the value of what biography contributes, the ethics of writing biography, and questions regarding whose narratives get preserved in a given culture and how can biographers locate the less-told stories of lives on the margins of a culture or society. One of the issues that biographers work with is the question of the extent to which a biography needs to be written as art or craft. How much artistic license can a biographer take and for what purpose? As several writers have pointed out, while it is important to move away from a rendering of "just the facts," which may leave the biography flat and devoid of life-breath, to fill it with imaginative speculations may well result in a distorted picture. The struggle with balance is related to the idea of "truth-telling" in biography. It is also related to the question of what new knowledge is generated by biographies? The challenge to biographies comes from postmodernism and poststructuralist critiques of selfhood. If the coherence of a self is imposed or constructed by narrative, then can any account of a life be considered anything other than fiction? While this challenge is important to understand, for life writers, the real issue is with figuring out what new depths or understandings of a life a biographer can uncover for the reader.

Ethical Issues

Ethical issues that concern biographical writing are centered on the responsibility and obligations of the biographer. A biographer writes about the life of persons who are deceased and who are no longer around to defend or explain their actions. Therefore the rights of a biographer often stem from permissions granted by the heirs or legal estate of the deceased to materials—documents and letters from which to craft the biography. The biographer working in archives is confronted with similar ethical issues as she chooses the material she will quote from or publish. McKee and Porter (2012) describe the decision made by Steve Lamos in his research on writing program administrators on what to include from the archives and what to exclude. Although some material helped him to better understand and "triangulate" his findings, he nevertheless excluded correspondence from an angry faculty member to the chancellor that he deemed "private" as opposed to minutes from faculty meetings that he classified as "public." His choice to use or not use such material was an ethical choice resulting from his research analysis and coding of materials into public and private.

Life writing researchers working in archives are likely to face similar types of ethical issues as those working with living participants. While participants who are alive can negotiate consent, with archival materials, the responsibility of figuring out the ethical nuances of what to make public and what to keep private are much more complex. Here are some likely scenarios that archival researchers will confront:

1. Did the person you wish to write about make all their materials freely available? If so, the decision regarding the "life" you wish to

write about comes from your own motivation and interest. Why this person? Why now? Reflecting on these questions will help you to figure out a logical rationale that goes beyond generalities regarding adding to the knowledge base in the field.

2. What is missing from the life writings that are available? Why is this the case? This question will help you determine what pieces are missing and whether those are important to your questions and research.

3. Are you using the materials in a way that does not distort what the writer intended? Researcher interpretations can sometimes lead to different outcomes. It is important that the researcher be transparent about the process of interpretation, a component of reflexivity.

4. Whom to ask for permission in case the archival material is "by permission only"? Typically, there will be either an estate, heirs, or a person or institution who "owns" the material in the archives. As a life writing researcher, you will need to contact the people concerned to ask for permission to use the archival material.

5. Once you have access to the archival material, you will need to figure out what you wish to use, what should remain perhaps private, and what can be made public through a publication. The ethics of a researcher come into play with regard to this decision-making process. Should the privacy of the person be revealed? What would be a good reason for such revelations?

6. Ponder the pros and cons of being an artist versus a craftsman and whether such a dichotomy is necessary within biographical projects that use archives.

Research Journal and Sketchbook Exercise 6

Use the sets of questions/propositions above and write your responses, then share them with another life writer and compare your responses with one another.

Life writers often use biography as a way to engage with their subject. As scholars of biographical writing have noted, in the quest for biography, at times, when relevant records have been hard to find, biographers have had to search for fragments of information found in different sources, not unlike notes in margins. Hudson (2009), in writing about the life of Mary Ellen Pleasant, is a case in point. Hudson found too few records of Pleasant, with most of those being privately owned. Hudson (2009) describes the different groups of people interested in preserving Pleasant's memory. As biographers engaging with a person's life, we need to understand who or which group wants to preserve a particular type of memory or image and the reasons for doing the same. Lieblich (2004) points out that self-interest often dictates what people choose to tell a biographer. Hudson (2009) extends that idea to explain that the interests of people living in the present can at times illuminate how the past is either preserved, reviled, or presented. Hudson (2009), in trying to piece together the life of Pleasant, realized that since sources were limited, imagination rushed to fill that void in the form of fictional accounts of Pleasant's life that became popular and in turn popularized the historical figure. While biographers often resist the critique offered by postmodernism and worry that the genre of biography is taken over other forms of life writing, Hudson (2009) reminds us that biographers are limited by their sources when trying to "re-imagine a life in a time not our own." In doing so, "efforts to control that imagination, or insist on one version of it miss the point entirely" (p. 222). Lieblich (2004) argues that the ultimate truth is out of reach for biographers and reminds biographers that just because a project is complete does not mean all sources are exhausted. She also discusses the part that randomness or luck and chance play in discoveries in the archives.

Research Journal and Sketchbook Exercise 7

1. Locate an artifact that you can use to tell a story about yourself; specifically a story about your educational journey.
2. Record your telling of this story as an audio file or podcast.
3. Take a photo or draw a picture or paint a picture of your artifact.

4. Ask someone who knows you to tell a story about you by looking at your artifact or a rendering of that artifact that you drew, painted, or photographed.
5. Then write in your RJ/SB a comparison of the story you told using the artifact and the story someone else told about you using the same artifact.

Autobiography

Autobiography has always been a site for interrogation of "self"; how a person comes to an understanding of themselves in relation to their surrounding context and decides to narrate a story about themselves. What some life writing scholars refer to as the "biographical turn" represents an important collection of historical markers that show the spectrum of different academic disciplines, all approaching new understandings of the self. Feminist epistemologies helped frame new forms of autobiography. Notable works such as May Sarton's *Journal of a Solitude* (1973) and Mary Catherine Bateson's *Composing a Life* (1990) and *Composing a Further Life: The Age of Active Wisdom* (2011) were followed by works such as Ascher, DeSalvo, and Ruddick's *Between Women Biographers, Novelists, Critics, Teachers and Artists Write About Their Work on Women* (1993) alongside autobiography theorists such as Liz Stanley (1992), who used the term "auto/biography" as a way to symbolize the inescapable connection between autobiography and biography.

Within the evolution of life writing categories of autobiography and biography there are instances where a slash was inserted in the following way: auto/biography. This visual interruption and rejoining of the two dimensions of the term was more than just symbolic: "Auto/biographical: Being aware of the extent to which we use other's stories to make sense of our own biographies, as well as how we use our own to make sense of others' lives and experiences" (Merrill and West, 2009, p. 191). If we trace historical influences on autobiography, we can go as far back as Augustine's *Confessions* (398 CE) or Rousseau's book of the same name (1782). These autobiographies focused on the act of reflexivity, inwardness, and self-interpretation (Peterson, 1986). In 1987 Smith captured it well when she wrote, "autobiography criticism [has moved from a] preoccupation with the life (bios) to the self (autos), to the text (graphe) of the autobiographer" (Smith, 1987, p. 3).

Types within Autobiography

May Sarton, for example, was a very prolific life writer who wrote books in all types of genres, including journals, diaries, fiction, non-fiction, children's books, poetry, plays, and more. Reading the complete compendium of her works is instructive, as it allows a close examination of a whole variety of ways life writing can be arranged and written and pushes at conventional notions of autobiographical writing (Mulvihill, 2000).

Carolyn Heilbrun, a feminist professor who offered crucial theoretical re-framings for writing women's lives, also experimented with various life writing forms, including taking a pen name (i.e., Amanda Cross) when writing a series of mystery novels featuring a female professor (Kate Fansler) working to solve murders and other crimes within an academic setting. Heilbrun's work remains a seminal contribution to feminist life writing.

Mary Catherine Bateson, the daughter of Margaret Mead, contributed an important book entitled *Composing a Life* that offered a collective biography of high-profile women academics discussing with each other the ways in which they navigated their multiple personal and professional life decisions. This collective life writing project provided a compelling model for others wishing to experiment with bringing various lives into conversation with each other. And Liz Stanley (1992) introduced the term "auto/biography" (with a slash) in order to draw attention to

> the interrelationship between the constructions of our own lives through autobiography and the construction of others' lives through biography. We cannot, in a sense, write stories

of others without reflecting our own histories, social and cultural locations as well as subjectivities and values.

(Merrill and West, 2009, p. 5)

Research Journal and Sketchbook Exercise 8

Read a biography or autobiography.

1. Why did you select it?
2. What were the most memorable aspects of this biography [or autobiography]? And why?
3. How would you describe the author's process? How did they arrange the narrative? What were the data sources? Were the data sources present in the writing? Did they interpret the data? Can you identify the methodology? Can you trace the methods used?
4. Was it a satisfying read? Why or why not?
5. Draw the cover art provided. Then draw an alternative cover from your own imagination. Describe the difference and what meanings are highlighted by each version.

Memory, Memoir, and Autobiographical Life Writing

The role of memory in life writing is both challenged and reified at the same time. How much one can depend on memory in life writing is challenged by Mary Gordon's (1996) book on her father and the process by which she learns about her father. In her approach to life writing, she acts like a detective—she depends on research to "dig up the past." She begins with what she believes she knows about her father—that he was a Catholic, had been at Harvard and France, a man whom she had loved, and it was this desire to learn more about him that started her on her quest. However, as she puts it, her "cave of memory" turned out to be a "tourist trap." In the process of her digging up the past, she learns that her father was not Catholic as she had previously believed, but was Jewish. In her writing, Gordon reveals her struggle with her sense of betrayal, her effort to adjust her image of her father to the new knowledge she discovered about him, and her eventual understanding of herself as separate from her father. Her dependence on research to gather facts rather than rely on false memories or even her father's depictions of himself reveal a mistrust of memory as a sole source life writing. Her writing is therefore a process of detection; she searches for his life among the documents of his life and she admits to feeling like "a detective in the department of magical realism" (Gordon, 1996, p. xxii). She writes of how she tracks him down in several archives, and each search reveals a new man, a different father than the one she remembered. She also reveals a struggle with herself, as she works to figure out why she needs to uncover the truth that her father worked so hard to conceal. This last is also an ethical question to herself, a question not unlike one that comes up in the work of Lorna Sage's Bad Blood (2000). Sage (2000) writes her life as an escape from the suffocating environment of her youth, and she explores her family history by examining the private diaries of her grandfather, an Anglican priest whose affairs with the district nurse and a seventeen-year-old friend of his granddaughter were documented.

Sara Wheeler (2004) discusses the "polar gap" between two pieces of evidence. She underscores the unreliability of memory as she describes Angela, the widow of Apsley Cherry-Garrard, the author of "The Worst Journey in the World." Angela recounts a story to Wheeler about her neighbors from half a century ago and the rage of her husband at the piano playing of the Russell family (Bertrand, Patricia, and Conrad). Wheeler wrote to Conrad to inquire if he remembered his "grumpy neighbor" to which Conrad Russell, now the fifth Earl, not only responded but added that "we never owned a piano." In the absence of this note, Wheeler speculates that she would have been tempted to treat memory as reliable evidence, raising the question of what is factual or not.

Autoethnography

Autoethnography is a form of life writing that has captured the interest and imagination of a growing number of social science scholars.

Autoethnography is a burgeoning area of research and includes a variety of innovative methods. Hughes, Pennington, and Makris (2012) offer the etymology of the word as a way to capture a fuller understanding of the hybrid nature of the term:

> The term *auto* is commonly used in the academy when referencing publications in which the author presents critical reflections and interpretations of personal experience. In contrast, *ethnography* is commonly referenced as a key qualitative approach to studying the rules, norms, and acts of resistance associated with cultural groups. Consequently, the hybrid term, *autoethnography*, is intended to name a form of critical self-study in which the researcher takes an active, scientific, and systematic view of personal experience in relation to cultural groups identified by the researcher as similar to the *self*. . . or as *others* who differ from the self.
>
> (Hughes et al., 2012, p. 209)

Perhaps, however, the most succinct and clarifying description of autoethnography as a form of life writing can be found in an article authored by Ellis, Adams, and Bochner (2010) published within the *Forum: Qualitative Social Research* (FQS):

> Autoethnography is an approach to research and writing that seeks to describe and systematically analyze (*graphy*) personal experience (*auto*) in order to understand cultural experience (*ethno*) (Ellis, 2004; Holman Jones, 2005). This approach challenges canonical ways of doing research and representing others (Spry, 2001) and treats research as a political, socially-just and socially-conscious act (Adams and Holman Jones, 2008). A researcher uses tenets of *autobiography* and *ethnography* to *do* and *write* autoethnography. Thus, as a method, autoethnography is both process and product.
>
> (Ellis, Adams, and Bochner, 2011, p. 1. Emphasis in original.)

Carolyn Ellis, with a background in Communication Studies, and Laurel Richardson, a Sociologist, carved the early pathways for auto-ethnography by pushing back the weeds that muted the reflexive

"I" and charted new directions for understanding the social context within which the self develops. This form of life writing grapples with the subcultures that cull together people with similarities. Auto-ethnographies are interested in the interaction between the subculture, and the sub-groups it constitutes, and how the personal and cultural experiences intermingle. The researcher is a self-identified insider to the group/subculture they identify as worthy of study and engage in life writing from that unique vantage point.

Tami Spry, Tony Adams, Stacy Holman Jones, Anne Harris, Joe Norris, and others helped to further diversify this form of life writing. Tami Spry uses autoethnographic performance as a method of inquiry (Spry, 2001; 2011) and Adams, Holman Jones, and Ellis served as editors for the much acclaimed *Handbook of Autoethnography* filled with 34 chapters, each shaping a new dimension of the possibilities for autoethnographic work, including a host of exemplars. For example, Stacy Holman Jones characterized auto-ethnography as

> working at the intersections of performance and ethnography [and] understanding fieldwork as personal and knowledge as embodied, critical, and [as an] ethical exploration of culture . . . [which] offers us a powerful form for theorizing the daily workings of culture.
>
> (Holman Jones, Adams, and Ellis, 2013, p. 19)

And Ellis and Adams collaborated on a chapter in Patricia Levy's edited *Oxford Handbook of Qualitative Research* (2014), crafting an account of "the purposes, practices, and principles, of autoethnographic research" (pp. 254–276), taking up again the essential questions of the expanding field. Anne Harris, playwright and critical autoethnographer, is pushing the boundaries of performance studies, and Joe Norris continues to create new permutations of duoethnography.

An important distinction between ethnography and autoethnography relates to the status of "insider" in a study. While an ethnographer strives to become an insider, an autoethnographer is the insider. In an autoethnography, the goal is to externalize the inner experiences of the autoethnographer while connecting it to social issues or questions that relate to the social world one inhabits. It allows marginalized populations to tell their own stories instead of being cast as the "exotic other" in ethnographic accounts. Autoethnography becomes research when the writer's story connects to the social structure (Denzin, 2006). In 2016, Arthur P. Bochner and Carolyn Ellis traced the evolution of autoethnography and documented the pronounced impact the annual International Congress of Qualitative Inquiry (ICQI) had, and continues to have, on autoethnography as a qualitative inquiry form of life writing. Bochner and Ellis, pioneers themselves in the tale of carving new paths for autoethnography, trace this form of life writing first as a "form of indigenous ethnography, through its inception as a mode of resistance to conventional ethnographic writing practices and silent authorship, to its introduction as a narrative identity and covering term" (Bochner and Ellis, 2016a, p. 208). They recount the early days of their own work when they were considering how to name the new form of life writing as it was emerging in their projects. Scanning the terrain of the literature they considered "personal essay (Krieger, 1991), socioautobiography (Zola, 1982), confessional tale (Van Maanen, 1988), ethnographic autobiography (Brandes, 1982), self-ethnography (Caughey, 1982), or personal ethnography (Crawford, 1996)" (Bochner and Ellis, 2016a, p. 210), but instead used terms such as "first-person account" and "evocative narrative," and then later Ellis used "emotional sociology," "evocation," and "autobiographical sociology" as the larger field of qualitative inquiry was heading toward the "narrative turn." Ellis and Bochner were leading the way toward a meta-cognition about these various forms of life writing and identified autoethnography as a "genre under which many species of autobiographical narrative and self-ethnography could fall" (Bochner and Ellis, 2016a, p. 211).

Types of Autoethnography

Below we provide brief descriptions of the various types of autoethnography in order to identify the unifying threads of this approach to life writing while honoring the distinctions between each type.

Evocative and Analytic

Several types of autoethnography have developed over the years, with two main strands that have proved popular—the analytic and evocative. Both types have a few distinctive features with their supporters and critics. Evocative autoethnography, according to Ellis and Bochner (2000; 2016b), is a methodology and is "akin to the novel or biography and thus fractures the boundaries that normally separate social science from literature"(p. 744). Analytic autoethnography (Anderson, 2006) emphasizes realist autoethnography that is theoretical and where the understanding of self is connected to an ethnographic context. Analytic autoethnography is regarded as more traditional in its description and location of the self in the narrative. Postmodern scholars (Ellis and Bochner, 2006) critique analytic autoethnography as too traditional and argue that autoethnography is meant to blur boundaries and be creative through the use of personal, evocative writing. Evocative autoethnographical writing has consequently ranged from poetry to art and stories as ways of storying the self. Eschewing this dichotomy and divide between the analytic and evocative autoethnography, Tedlock (2013) suggests "braiding evocative with analytic autoethnography" (p. 358). Calling for a combination of the two, she argues that narratives can invoke emotions while being analytical and offers a few examples of autoethnographies that have successfully "braided" the two. These include Minge (2013), who combined visual arts and photography with an analysis to tell family stories. Others who work in this genre include Tillman (2013), who weaves personal narrative into the history of racism and homophobia in the United States and mixes analytic and evocative autoethnography.

Performative Autoethnography

Tami Spry uses autoethnographic performance to create and share new methods of life writing. Spry writes about performing autoethnography as a "concentrating on the body as the site from which the story is generated" (Spry, 2001, p. 708). She identified this life writing approach as "a vehicle of emancipation from cultural and familial identity scripts" (Spry, 2001, p. 708) and a means to "dialogically look back upon myself as other, generating critical agency in the stories of my life, as the polyglot facets of self and other engage, interrogate, and embrace" (Spry, 2001, p. 708).

Anna Deavere Smith—professor, artist, actress, playwright, and founding director of the Institute of the Arts and Civic Dialogue—creates live performances derived from ethnographic fieldnotes, interviews, artifacts, and at times autoethnographic research. Her theatrical performances are perhaps the most sophisticated translations of oral history and ethnographic observations that have yet to be created and performed for audiences around the world. Her most recent project explored the school-to-prison pipeline, referred to as the Pipeline Project (2016). To get a glimpse of Anna Deavere Smith's performative, autoethnographic, life writing work, look at the following:

> https://www.ted.com/talks/anna_deavere_smith_s_american_
>   character?language=en
> http://annadeaveresmithprojects.net/

And Brydie-Leigh Bartleet provides an overview of additional forms of autoethnographic life writing and representations as created by the use of various artistic mediums, not just theatrical performance, but also drama, visual arts, dance, paintings, music, film, etc. (Bartleet, 2013).

Critical Autoethnography

Boylorn and Orbe (2016) have curated an edited collection of chapters examining the autoethnographic forms of life writing that emerge when constructed from a critical theory perspective. They have placed a focus on an "intersectional analysis [that] looks at self-identifications, social identifications, and cultural signifiers . . . to interrogate how overlapping and seemingly opposing identity affiliations influence our personal lives, relationships, and narratives" (Boylorn and Orbe, 2016, p. 235). Stacey Holman Jones's work moves the needle forward on situating the contributions critical theory makes to autoethnography:

> The "critical" in critical autoethnography reminds us that theory is not a static or autonomous set of ideas, objects, or

practices. Instead, theorizing is an ongoing process that links the concrete and abstract, thinking and acting, aesthetics, and criticism in what performance studies scholar Della Pollock describes as "living bodies of thought"

(Holman Jones, 2016, p. 228)

Understanding critical ethnography as cultural analysis through personal narrative opens up numerous possibilities for life writing projects.

Collaborative Autoethnography

Collaborative autoethnography is another type of autoethnographic life writing that is pushing at the artificial boundaries of how we create and share stories that illuminate the social structures around which individual lives and groups of individuals claim agency and voice. Collaborative autoethnography is "a qualitative research method in which researchers work in community to collect their autobiographical materials and to analyze and interpret their data collectively to gain a meaningful understanding of sociocultural phenomena reflected in their autobiographical data" (Chang, Ngunjiri, and Hernandez, 2012, pp. 23–24). Chang and others remind us that the researcher is "simultaneously the instrument and the data source" (Chang et al., 2012, p. 22). Collaborations of many forms are producing a rich array of autoethnographic life writing and Garbati and Rothschild (2016) provide advice to all interested in pursuing this type of life writing project when they say:

> Although the CAE methods have some variations, all involve researchers individually and collaboratively reflecting upon a particular phenomenon. An important aspect of CAE is for researchers to remain flexible and open-minded about the direction of the study and to document progress.
>
> (Garbati and Rothschild, 2016, p. 4)

Duoethnography is another closely related form of life writing relying on collaboration among two (or more) researchers. Sawyer and Norris describe duoethnography as placing life histories, or life stories (select portions of life histories), in conversation in order to elevate collective understandings of how the social world shapes lives (Sawyer and Norris, 2013). Data collection methods used for duoethnographies are characterized by an iterative process whereby the "emphasis is on the revisiting of the data throughout the research process as participants share and reflect on their personal contributions to the data set" (Garbati and Rothschild, 2016, p. 5).

Autoethnography has deep methodological roots and is a mode of life writing that has its origins in traditional anthropological versions of ethnography. Malinowski and Mead exemplify anthropologists traveling to exotic lands where they lived with their subjects while trying to become insiders in a society that was unfamiliar to them. Ethnography, over time, moved away from the "exotic" and instead identified cultural questions related to the everyday common experiences found in schools, institutions, or dance halls. Autoethnography is still a relatively newer form of life writing that validates personal experiences and connects the personal with the political. It represents the "fifth moment" in qualitative research as described by Denzin and Lincoln (2005) and has a history of using critical, social justice-oriented theories.

Reading a range of autoethnographies can give researchers an overview of the possibilities since some writers have painstakingly documented their experiences and shared highly transparent methodological insights. For example, the evocative life writing by Paulette (1993) titled "A Choice for K'ailia" is the personal recounting of a parent's difficult dilemma and subsequent decisions regarding her infant son's terminal illness. The narrative recounts a unique perspective that is rarely brought to light. A feminist autoethnography that exemplifies the phrase "the personal is the political" is the story told by Paige Averett (2009), whose attempt to understand her own relationship to men through an art project led her to search for the figure of "Wonder Woman" in toy stores. The absence of "Wonder Woman" and indeed, for that matter, any figure that represented a strong, action-oriented woman or a woman as a superhero were absent from stores, leading Averett to reflect on patriarchy and its control over the role models that were available to young girls and women. Her article relates how she uses her own autoethnography to teach graduate students to write theirs, leading them to see how their personal experiences were tied to the larger social structures in which we live. Averett's (2009) account of autoethnography is an example of a story that is firmly grounded in feminist theory. She does not tell us whether she had any trouble getting the account published, and we can perhaps assume that her theoretical framework was enough to satisfy reviewers. Other autoethnographers, for example, Sparkes (2000) and Holt (2003), describe the issues they had trying to publish autoethnographies. They describe reviewers' comments regarding the need for traditionally academic-oriented writing. In their case, reviewers wanted to see an audit trail, descriptions of more traditional methodology.

Autoethnography is located by researchers within a postmodern framework as they describe the emancipatory potential of autoethnography in its push against the traditional positivist paradigms. Criticisms leveled against autoethnography are focused on their very characteristics. For example, in an autoethnography, the self is the subject of the inquiry or story. For critics of this type of life writing, the focus on the "self" amounts to a narcissistic obsession (Atkinson, 1997). In addition, the focus on the self is also seen as devoid of context, what Atkinson termed an "absence of social context, social action and social interaction" (p. 339). Bochner (2001) refuted the charge that a focus on the self is decontextualized by pointing out that individuals are located in the social and cultural milieu and that their voices are similarly embedded in that social framework. Rich meaning, culturally relevant personal experience, and a motivation to know and understand experience strengthen autoethnography projects. These are just some of the examples of the directions life writers can take. They represent the continual evolution of autoethnographic life writing and may provide inspiration for your own life writing projects.

Research Journal and Sketchbook Exercise 9

Use Table 2.1 to brainstorm some ideas about possible projects you might design using each of these various forms of auto-ethnography. This thought-experiment might help you build a conceptual model of how these various types of autoethnography have common threads, yet each are distinct.

TABLE 2.1 Types of Autoethnography

Type→ Planning Notes↓	Evocative	Analytic	Braided (Analytic and Evocative)	Performative	Critical	Collaborative	Duoethnography
What group/sub-group membership(s) do I hold that make me an insider to some set of experiences? How would these help me think about this type of autoethnography?							
What research questions (RQs) am I most interested in exploring?							
What methodological literature would help me organize this type of autoethnography?							
What data collection methods would I employ for this type of autoethnography?							

Life History

Life history, as an approach to life writing, is often constructed chronologically, although some life writers reject organizing the narrative in that way. Life histories are commonplace in the medical and allied-health professions and are often referred to as "patient history," "medical history," "health history," or "case notes." These versions of life history writing require the person to provide a themed version of their life story guided by the prompts/questions detailing their health history. Life history is also a term used by biologists interested in charting the evolution of different life forms.

Social scientists, sociologists in particular, have long been interested in chronological timelines and associated stories over the course of the entire life. Others have experimented with life history narratives for different purposes. For example, Sandra G. Kouritzin (2000) wrote about the one-time neglect of life history within the educational research methodology literature and put forth a methodological treatment of the approach in her own work within the context of English as a Second Language (ESL). She provided five categories for ways scholars think about life history:

1. A theoretical and methodological frame
2. A type of social science interview
3. The topic or technique used in obtaining linguistic samples (fairly common in the ESL context)
4. A pedagogical approach drawing on life experiences
5. A specific measurable variable (e.g., years of education, socioeconomic status, place of birth, length of residence in Canada).

(Kouritzin, 2000, p. 3)

Kouritzin also offers the following distinction between a life history approach and other approaches to life writing:

> Although the case study might be concerned with documenting the immediate physical and emotional context, and may do so over time, life history research focuses on individuals' understanding and recollection of events that have had a

substantial impact on their development. To achieve these ends, the life history may employ (a) oral accounts of the participant's life narrated by the participant, (b) interview data used to flesh out and to aid in understanding the oral history, (c) any available documents (e.g. diaries, letters, school records, legal papers, news clippings) corroborating or contradicting the narrator's life events, (d) third-party interviews with other persons to provide additional information or alternative interpretations, (e) reference and comparison with other research and examples, and (f) analysis and comparison across the different sources. This can roughly be categorized as three orders of data: the first-party report (a&b), the third-party report (c&d), and the researcher report (e&f), with the nucleus being an oral life story narration. . . . The emphasis on oral narration has particular importance in life history because it necessitates the presence of the Other who both summons the performance of storytelling and collaborates in conjuring the context. The designation life history may be misleading because it implies that the story encompasses a lifetime when it may center on a particular time frame, event, or focus [rather] than the entire story of one's life.

(Kouritzin, 2000, pp. 4–6)

The roots of life history can be traced back to the 1920s when anthropologists used life history approaches to describe Native American cultures (Radin, 1926). In 1927, the seminal work of Thomas and Znaniecki was published, and it was a sociological life history entitled, *The Polish Peasant in Europe and America*. The 1930s saw a blending between disciplines of anthropology and psychology that brought into being a life history analysis (Sapir, 1932). Dollard (1949) published *Criteria for the Life History*, which attempted to integrate the study of culture with psychoanalysis. Long (1999) noted the overwhelming emphasis in life histories in the classic sociological literature and sought to redress the absence of women by examining the rare life histories of women. One of them, *Boxcar Bertha*, written in the 1930s, in sharp contrast to male life histories, has a silent and invisible narrator, and it is Bertha's voice that is a strong first-person voice. Nevertheless, the silent narrator exists and Bertha's life history was first published as *Sister of the Road as told to Dr. Ben Reitman.*

Berg and Lune (2012) view life history as within historiographic methods where the life history interview is a variation of a depth interview. Atkinson's (1998) reference to a life story is similar to a life history narrative. A life history is the story of one person whose story the researcher wants to tell. The life history may be that of a person who is living an ordinary life, but their experiences and stories make for rich data and present a unique contribution towards helping us understand culture.

Life history was often subsumed within narrative approaches to qualitative research. Hatch and Wisniewski (1995) gathered, through a survey, different scholars' views on the distinction between life history and narrative. Lincoln (Hatch and Wisniewski, 1995) provides an example of the type of distinction that scholars made between the two terms. These authors say, "life history is always the history of a life, a single life, told from a particular vantage point, while narrative may be a style of telling, a particular way of constructing the story of several individuals or a group" (p. 115).

The term life history was often used with the term narrative so that life history narrative was used to mean oral history, informal narratives, personal narratives, and life stories. Over time, each of these has emerged as a distinct type of life writing and yet all of them have at their center the lives of persons. Pauline Chinn (1995) added context to this definition by asserting that, in life history, the life writer constructs a story of an individual "historically situated in culture, time and place" (p. 115). Other definitions include life history as "any retrospective account by the individual of his/her life . . . elicited or prompted by another person" (Watson and Watson-Franke, 1985, p. 2) or as "sociologically read biography" (Measor and Sikes, 1992, p. 210).

Plummer (2001) outlined three types of life histories. He distinguished between life histories that are "naturalistic" or stories of lives told as part of cultural transmission and life histories that are specifically researched. Cultural stories told within a culture would be stories of mythic figures or heroic figures or events passed on orally in cultural groups. Life histories that are researched have researchers play a significant role as they attempt to gather new information. He also mentions a third type of life history that is a "reflexive" life history, or one constructed self-consciously while engaging with reflexivity. This type of life history bends closer to autobiography or autoethnography.

Frank (1979) suggests that a life history is the product of the collaboration between the researcher and the subject, with the researcher querying, 'How does this person compare to ourselves?' Life histories are texts that combine the consciousness of the subject and the researcher, making such texts silhouettes of the researcher as much as life histories of the subject. Kohli (1981) suggested life histories are "structured self-images" while Ferrarotti (1983) defined a life history as a story from below. In other words, life histories offered a counterstory to the dominant viewpoint. Bertaux (1981) describes a life history as a life story that includes other data sources besides an oral account of a person's own life.

Judy Long (1999) distinguished between a life history and autobiography by pointing out that a life history is in some ways similar or comparable to an autobiography. Long (1999) claims that the similarities should not distract us from the distinctive nature of life history as it differs in important ways. Unlike autobiography, which can be a participant/subject's conversation with oneself, a life history originates "reactively, rather than spontaneously" (p. 73). By this, Long means that the role of the narrator in life history is central to the account. Participants relate their life history in response to the questions and interests raised by the narrator. In addition, as Long (1999) points out, the participant not only has a relationship with the visible face-to-face narrator, but also one with an audience whom she will never know. The narrator or the researcher in turn is involved with the participant in a bounded time frame but is also building a relationship with her professional peers, readership, and audience. Becker (1966) and Long (1999) have described the role of the sociologist in shaping the narratives in life history. While Becker (1966) says that the narrator or researcher is oriented to questions raised by sociologists and shapes the work for sociological ends, Long (1999) points us to the power of the researcher in the relationship with the participant. Since life history is often written in the first-person voice, the unseen narrator's role in shaping that narrative is central to understanding life history as a method of life writing. The relationship between the participant and researcher is central to how the story is shaped and told and is often affected by gender, race, class and disability, and sexuality.

Long's (1999) contribution to life history research makes possible new configurations of the subject, narrator, reader, and text. Transformed by feminist writings and conceptualized as a counter to traditional sociological life histories, Long explains the S/N/R/T framework as providing a forward momentum. It is through reflexivity that a researcher is transformed into a narrator. Long uses the term "narrator" to describe a researcher who exercises reflexivity so that the subjectivity of the researcher is brought into the frame of analysis as much as the text or the participant's stories. Reflexivity treats feelings as important and as information to be considered. It does not mean losing oneself in feelings and emotions as much as it means restoring feelings to the context so that an informed analysis can take place. The life history narrative within the S/N/R/T framework works to understand connections and affinities, interactions, and interpersonal dynamics. Long's work was significant in reconciling the various forms of life writing being produced by sociologists, historians, and other social scientists steeped in their disciplinary traditions but blinded by the interdisciplinary opportunities. In particular, the interdisciplinary approach opened up new spaces to better represent the lives of women and other underrepresented populations rarely at the center of life writing projects by academics.

In life history writing, the relationship between the participant and the researcher is central. Life histories are often collaborative endeavors. The encounter between the researcher and the participant is an important one in life writing, and this is true for life history research. Knowles (2001) describes the similarities between his experiences and that of Thomas with whom he collaborated to write the life history of Thomas. Knowles (2001) says that the "revelation of Thomas's life is a representation of my own as well" (p. 2), thereby acknowledging the collaborative nature of the work as well as the dual consciousness that had to come together for the life history to work. Knowles (2001) characterizes the interviews with Thomas as "conversations" and acknowledges his responsibility for the analyses and his viewing of Thomas through his own experiences. He says, "I have made meaning of his experiences through the lenses of my own life experiences and perspectives" (p. 4). By saying this, Knowles (2001) refers to a point repeatedly made in qualitative research—that the researcher is the instrument of research (Bogdan and Biklen, 2007). Therefore, the researchers' own frame of reference, personal autobiography, and experiences all play a role in the analyses and representation, a point that is clarified and honed through exercises in reflexivity.

Bertaux and Kohli (1984) drew a distinction between interpretive and scientific approaches to life histories. According to them, the former has as its focus the individual life story and the latter's purpose is to uncover patterns of social relations. But for others the narrative in life history research can be constructed as a novel, a short story, or a fairy tale (Riessman, 2003). A novel would mean an exhaustive life history that examines the participant's whole life, a short story would focus on key events in the participant's life, and a fairy tale would be constructed out of specific themes in a person's life. One of the earliest examples of life history is the book co-authored by Thomas and Zanecki (1918) called *The Polish Peasant in Europe and America*. This is an example of a *sociological* life history. And so is *The Jack Roller* (Bruce and Shaw, 1930), a sociological autobiographical life history of a delinquent youth. *Black Elk Speaks* (Neihardt, 1932/2008) and *Nisa: The Life and Words of a !Kung Woman* by Marjorie Shostack (1981) are often-cited examples of a traditional anthropological life history.

While a life history typically takes time, a focused life history using a topical interview is a way of conducting a life history and gathering data in shorter periods. According to Shopes (2011):

> Life history interviews, often undertaken within local or community settings, record a narrator's biography, addressing topics such as family life; educational and work experiences; social, political and religious involvements; and, at their best, the relationship of personal history to broader historical events and social themes.
>
> (p. 452)

Choosing a Participant for Life History Projects

In life history research, often, a participant is already known to the researcher. An interest in learning about a person's experiences may be the primary motivator. Approaching a participant with a view to conducting a life history represents a commitment on the part of both the researcher and the participant, and it involves embarking on a long-term research relationship. While some life histories may be short-term projects, they are nevertheless intense and collaborative. The choice of a participant needs to be thought through by the researcher carefully. Some degree of shared experiences or an interest in learning about the comparative differences the two experiences can lead to a choice of participant for the life history research. Data-gathering methods also need careful consideration. A predominant method for conducting research in life history is the interview. Life history interviews, although sharing characteristics of generic interviews adopted by most qualitative researchers, tend to be longer and more in-depth. The role of the researcher is one of a listener, trying to be minimalist with verbal prompts, while the participant, or narrator, interprets their life. Questions for life history interviews often take the form of broad yet challenging queries. A question that can be used for whole-life kinds of life history interviews, rather than bounded-life history interviews, is: "If your life were a book, what would the chapters be called?" This type of question prompts the person to place some framework of meaning on their life history and, within that structure, they can move forward and backward between the chapter titles to tell stories. In so doing, they can create another layer of meaningful connections between the ways they have apportioned their life story.

Research Journal and Sketchbook Exercise 10

1. Try writing a mini-version of your life history by using this prompt:
    If your life were a book, what would the chapters be called?
2. Ask one other person to use the same prompt to tell you about their life history.
3. Then write an analytic memo reflecting on what you both created, including developing a new set of interview

> questions you might use as follow-up questions to probe for further nuanced meaning within both your self-narration and the narration of the person you selected to engage in a life history dialogue.

Besides interviews, like most forms of life writing, life history also draws on a variety of "life documents" (Plummer, 2001) to understand and construct life histories. Diaries, journals, photographs, videos, mementos, and artifacts can all be used to build life histories. They may serve as talismans, memory-holders, and/or documentation of essentials elements of a narrated story.

Research Journal and Sketchbook Exercise 11

1. Make a list of items that might be helpful if used within a process to help you elicit your own life history. Use Table 2.2 to help you jot some preliminary notes:

TABLE 2.2 Life Documents as Life History Prompts

Document Types→	Diary Entries	Journal Entries	Photographs	Videos	Momentos	Artifacts
Chapter Titles of Your Life History↓						

2. Now ask the person you prompted before to complete the same exercise.
3. Consider what new questions you might ask in the presence of these documents and create that new list.

Data Analysis in Life History

Data analysis in life history research can be similar to qualitative analyses using coding (Saldana, 2013). In the life history genre, Noblit and Hare (1988) suggest "translation" as one of the important steps in analysis. By "translation," they mean a synthesis of the account or accounts by participants to allow a comparison across and within such accounts. One challenge in life history research is how the participant views life history. On the one hand, the researcher may be intent on preserving confidentiality and privacy while, on the other hand, the participant may want the story to be acknowledged by readers and listeners. One of the challenges for researchers is figuring out what stories to hold back and what stories to tell through writing. The participants may also want to hold back some stories and not want them published or may want to edit their stories before publication.

The three issues of voice, authorship, and ownership need to be tackled in the life history approaches to life writing. Whose voice is being privileged and prioritized? Who owns the story and whose story is being told? Who is the ultimate author of the life history?

In life history method these issues are particularly problematic. Voice in life history is different from voice in autobiography or biography. Unlike autobiography, where the first person is used to narrate the story, and biography, where the third person is used for narrations, in life history, which is the story told by a participant to a researcher, the narrative is often told as a first-person account. These issues have been wrestled with by several scholars who have differing viewpoints.

Oral History

Feminism and oral history practices pushed life writers to "elicit and analyze the spoken and written records of people . . . who had been neglected in the mainstream social and historical record" (Merrill and West, 2009, p. 3). Studs Terkel's oral histories of ordinary people are examples of presenting the experiences of people who had been neglected by official historical records (Terkel, 1974).

Oral history is as a way of collecting, interpreting, and accentuating human experiences. Shopes, former president of the U.S. Oral History Association, offers this definition:

> [Oral history] can refer to recorded speech of any kind or to talking about the past in ways ranging from casual reminiscing among family members, neighbors, or coworkers to ritualized accounts presented in formal setting by culturally sanctioned tradition-bearers. Most typically, the term refers to what folklorists call personal experience narratives.
>
> (Shopes, 2011, p. 451)

And, Shopes suggests six defining characteristics of oral history practices:

1. "It is *first* an interview . . . it is not simply someone telling a story; it is someone telling a story in response to the queries of another; it is this dialogue that shapes the interview."
2. "*Second*, oral history is recorded, preserved for the record, and made accessible to others for a variety of uses."
3. "*Third*, oral history interviewing is historical in intent; that is, it seeks new knowledge about and insights into the past through individual biography. Although it always represents an interplay between past and present, the individual and the social, oral history is grounded in historical questions and hence requires that the interviewer has knowledge of both the subject at hand and the interviewee's relationship to that subject."
4. "*Fourth*, oral history is understood as both act of memory and an inherently subjective account of the past."
5. "*Fifth*, an oral history interview is an inquiry in depth. It is not a casual or serendipitous conversation but a planned and scheduled, serious and searching exchange, one that seeks a detailed, expansive, and reflective account of the past."
6. "Finally, oral history is fundamentally oral, reflecting both the conventions and dynamics of the spoken word."

(Shopes, 2011, pp. 451–452)

The Oral History Association's (OHA) *Principles and Best Practices for Oral History* (2009) "define standards governing the oral historian's relationship to the narrator, to standards of scholarship for history and related disciplines, and to both current and future users of the interview" (Shopes, 2011, p. 461).

Many qualitative researchers understand oral history projects as social justice projects and design their studies for that end. For example, Janesick (2007; 2010) has consistently worked to show the exciting intersections between oral history and critical qualitative methodologies that focus on social justice. And her productive use of choreography as a metaphor for the methodological movements associated with this form of life writing remains instructive (Mulvihill and Latz, 2011). Siobhan McHugh, a renowned oral historian, in *The Aerobic Art of Interviewing* (2007), recounts how the Italian oral historian, Alessandro Portelli, described interviews as "an exchange of gazes" (Portelli, 1997). McHugh is interested in how Portelli, and others, harnessed the concept of listening. When interviewing is understood to be a process of

> listening super-intently to every word . . . someone once termed it "aerobic listening." It is certainly exhausting in the way that listening in a conversation never is. The reason you do it is because your undivided attention is part of what causes the subject to open up. Few of us are ever really listened to in daily life . . . when someone REALLY listens to you, it's like a force field.
>
> (McHugh, 2007, p. 151)

McHugh shares the following to drive home this essential point:

> Michelangelo believed that a piece of marble already contained a work of art—his role was to liberate what was inherent. But the majesty, grace, and beauty he saw in the stone that became David remained invisible to sculptors who had previously tackled it. In a similar way, the interview can be all or nothing to writers, journalists, and oral historians. A person sits across a

table, with stories to tell, ideas to impart, facts to confirm or deny, perhaps a lifetime of emotions to convey—but our ability to perceive who is before us, and to engage with what we are hearing, will critically affect what ensues.

(McHugh, 2007, p. 147)

Making "word pictures" as an oral historian is a labor-intensive, yet satisfying, act of life writing and McHugh's reflections on her art and craft are filled with insights to help life writers who are making oral histories.

StoryCorps

StoryCorps is another great example of the powerful forms of oral history life writing.

In October 2003 StoryCorps opened a Story Booth inside Grand Central Station in New York City. According to their website:

> StoryCorps' mission is to preserve and share humanity's stories in order to build connections between people and create a more just and compassionate world. We do this to remind one another of our shared humanity, to strengthen and build the connections between people, to teach the value of listening, and to weave into the fabric of our culture the understanding that everyone's story matters. At the same time, we are creating an invaluable archive for future generations.
>
> (Retrieved from https://storycorps.org/about/)

> The core of the StoryCorps experience has always been the conversation. But sometimes, storytellers bring along photographs, mementos, family heirlooms, and other documents which are photographed and saved alongside the rest of the interview record.
>
> (Retrieved from https://storycorps.org/blog/fun-photos-a-look-at-what-participants-bring-to-the-booth/)

Research Journal and Sketchbook Exercise 12

1. Listen to a few of the entries on the StoryCorps website and write a memo about the voice tones and intonations you hear, about the flow of the narrative, and about the most memorable moments of the stories for you and why they impacted you.
2. Draw or sketch something in relation to the stories you listened to.

Groundswell Oral History Collective

The Groundswell Oral History Collective (www.oralhistoryfor socialchange.org/about/) is a "network of oral historians, activists, cultural workers, community organizers, and documentary artists that use oral history to further movement building and transformative social change" (www.oralhistoryforsocialchange.org/about/). Contained within their website are a tremendously rich set of tools for oral historians and examples of completed projects as well as an open bibliographic project where individuals can continue to add literature citations open to all interested in the nexus of oral history and social justice activism.

Research Journal and Sketchbook Exercise 13

Explore the Groundswell website and create a sketch of a concept map representing the intersecting dimensions of the resource sand projects they describe. And write a few paragraphs explaining your drawing.

Online repositories have made the storing and access of oral history data much easier than when one had to physically travel to places to examine documents in archives. Audio data of interviews are also available and, for the life writer, the opportunity to hear the inflections in tone and voice of the interviewer and the participant present exciting possibilities of analysis. Some collections of oral histories available online are: (a) audio recordings of interviews with elderly people from Columbus, Ohio about early life in the city (www.gcis.net/cjhs/oral.htm); and (b) Oral Histories of Kellytown located online at http://monticello.avenue.gen.va.us/Community/Neighborhoods/Kellytown/History.

Research Journal and Sketchbook Exercise 14

1. Interview one person in your family or neighborhood about their memories of life. Have them tell you about their childhood, adolescence, and life as an adult.

2. Interview a teenager in their late teens about her/his memories of childhood and about becoming a teenager.

   a. What differences do you see in the two oral history renderings? Pay particular attention to the stories and types of stories told by both people. What did you learn about oral history and interviewing from this exercise?

3. Locate an online repository designed for secondary data analysis and select a portion of the oral history data available. Then write an analytical memo about the life writing project ideas you might generate from that data set. For example, take a look at the following:

   a. Life Stories of Montrealers Displaced by War, Genocide, and other Human Rights Violations ("Montreal Life Stories") (www.lifestoriesmontreal.ca/)

   b. UK Data Archive (www.dataarchive.ac.uk/create-manage/consent-ethics)

   c. British Library (http://sounds.bl.uk/information/legal-and-ethical-usage)

   d. Oral History Society (www.ohs.org.uk/ethics/index.php)

As mentioned previously, interviewing is an essential component of oral history with memory and narration at its core. Oral historians often contemplate how to achieve high-quality sound with their recordings, how best to preserve the audio or video recordings, and whether to participate in an established repository or to create a repository of their own to store the audio or video recordings.

Research Journal and Sketchbook Exercise 15

1. Record an oral history interview using SoundCloud (*https://soundcloud.com/*) to practice with free software available to oral historians.
2. Write a list of pros and cons related to the questions about storing audio and/or video recordings within repositories and the potential for others to use the data to conduct a secondary data analysis project.

Data Analysis for Oral Histories

Subjectivity is an inescapable part of oral history interviewing. But instead of having the orientation that it is a condition to be guarded against, most life writers celebrate the subjectivity (rather than objectivity) of the constructed data. Oral histories where the interviewer is absent or where the questions are erased tell us little about the interview and create analytical problems. For example, it is difficult to know if the interviewer specifically requested some information or did not ask the interviewee to discuss certain issues. Revealing the questions in oral history interviewing represents the first layer in the analysis of data (Ritchie, 2003). In the case of the absent presence of the interviewer, it is difficult to analyze the assumptions of the interviewer in light of the interview. Similarly, if the questions reveal a vocal presence of the interviewer, it allows the researcher to analyze the types of questions asked and what they reveal about the assumptions and interests of the interviewer.

Since interviewees are often analyzing or interpreting their memories even while narrating them, there is a degree of analysis that takes place even during the data-gathering process.

In qualitative interviewing, researchers are often mindful of the power differential between the interviewer and the interviewee. In oral history, like much of life writing, power is shared between the interviewer and the respondent. In terms of the extent to which power is shared, the terms respondent, narrator, oral author, participant all show a degree of closeness, and the development of a relationship between the interviewer and the narrator. The term interviewee places the oral history interview as a one-sided endeavor, with the interviewer asking questions and the interviewee answering them. The sharing of power that is the hallmark of successful oral history methods is diminished if the interviewer and participant are not on par. The interviewer in oral history is often dependent on the participant for the quality and substantive nature of the data gathered. Oral historians have different views concerning data in oral history interviews. While some scholars prefer to work with transcripts rather than aural recordings, others believe that every transcription contains an element of analysis and interpretation on the part of the transcriber by way of cleaning up of dialects, pauses, or other voice modulations that are not noted in the transcripts.

Presenting Oral History

The end products of oral history can vary from papers and books on experiences of oral historians as they navigated their journeys from topic selection to interviewing and then analysis and writing. These writings may be biographies or stories or may even result in podcasts or documentary film. Life writers at times also present oral history results in some form to the community that participated in the research. Oral historians have produced many resources for life writers that convey the evolution of the methodological conversations and simultaneously provide the practical "how to" guidance (Perks and Thomson, 2006; Bornat and Diamond, 2007; Abrams, 2010). As Bornat (nd.) has discussed:

> While valuing the ensuing data for what it tells us about the past, oral historians also regard the interview as an object in

itself; it has a shape and totality determined not just by someone's life events but how that life is narrated and by the social relationship of the interview. [And] a growing interest in the social production of memory and the ways in which individual memory is able to co-exist with public and popular memorialising of the past.

(Bornatt, 2012)

Research Journal and Sketchbook Exercise 16

Oral History

1. Pick a friend or a family member to interview. This person should preferably be the "keeper of family lore."
2. Construct interview questions keeping in mind some questions you might want to know more about—for example, a particular period in her life or where she was and what she was doing during a series of historic moments, memories of her childhood, school playground and school classrooms.
3. Read an article or book that contextualizes politically, historically, and socially what you hear from your participant. For example, if your participant discusses what it was like to go to a recently desegregated school, read about the local history of schools and desegregation during the time period to which she is referring.

Moving forward, Chapter 3 will provide insights into some additional practical matters that may arise when working within any of these five approaches to life writing.

References

Abbott, H. P. (2008). *The Cambridge Introduction to Narrative*. Cambridge: Cambridge University Press.
Abrams, L. (2010). *Oral History Theory*. London: Routledge.

Adams, T. E., & Holman Jones, S. (2008). Autoethnography is queer. In *Handbook of Critical and Indigenous Methodologies* (pp. 373–390). Thousand Oaks, CA: Sage.

Anderson, L. (2006). Analytic autoethnography. *Journal of Contemporary Ethnography*, *35*(4), 373–395.

Antler, J. (1989). *Lucy Sprague Mitchell: The Making of a Modern Woman.* New Haven: Yale University Press.

Atkinson, P. (1997). Narrative turn or blind alley? *Qualitative Health Research*, 7, 325–344.

Atkinson, R. (1998). *The Life Story Interview.* Thousand Oaks, CA: Sage.

Averett, P. (2009). The search for Wonder Woman: An autoethnography of feminist identity. *Affilia: Journal of Women and Social Work*, *24*(4), 360–368.

Bartleet, B.-L. (2013). Artful and embodied methods, modes of inquiry, and forms of representation. In S. Holman Jones, Tony E. Adams, & Carolyn Ellis (Eds.), *Handbook of Autoethnography.* Walnut Creek, CA: Left Coast Press.

Bateson, M. C. (1990). *Composing a Life: Life as a Work in Progress—The Improvisations of Five Extraordinary Women.* New York: A Plum Book.

Bateson, M. C. (2011). *Composing a Further Life: The Age of Active Wisdom.* New York: Vintage Books.

Becker, H. S., Ed. (1966). *Social Problems: A Modern Approach.* Hoboken, NJ: J. Wiley and Sons.

Berg, B. L., & Lune, H. (2012). *Qualitative Research Methods for the Social Sciences* (8th ed.). New York: Pearson.

Bertaux, D., Ed. (1981). *Biography and Society.* Thousand Oaks, CA: Sage.

Bertaux, D., & Kohli, M. (1984). The life story approach. *Annual Review of Sociology*, *10*, 215–237.

Bochner, A. P. (2001). Narrative's virtues. *Qualitative Inquiry*, 7(2), 131–157.

Bochner, A. P., & Ellis, C. (Summer, 2016a). The ICQI and the rise of autoethnography: Solidarity through community. *International Review of Qualitative Research*, *9*(2), 208–217.

Bochner, A. P., & Ellis, C. (2016b). *Evocative Autoethnography: Writing Lives and Telling Stories.* New York: Routledge.

Bogdan, R., & Biklen, S. (2007). *Qualitative Research for Education: An Introduction to Theory and Practice.* New York: Pearson.

Bornat, J. (2012). Oral history and qualitative research, *Timescapes Methods Guides Series.* www.timescapes.leeds.ac.uk/assets/files/methods-guides/timescapes-bornat-oral-history.pdf

Bornat, J., & Diamond, H. (2007). Women's history and oral history: Developments and debates. *Women's History Review*, *16*(1), 19–39.

Bowen, G. A. (2009). Document analysis as a qualitative research method. *Qualitative Research Journal*, *9*(2), 27–40.

Boylorn, R. M., & Orbe, M. P., Eds. (2016). *Critical Autoethnography: Intersecting Cultural Identities in Everyday Life.* New York: Routledge.

Bruce, A. A., & Shaw, C. R. (1930). *The Jack-Roller*. Chicago: University of Chicago Press.

Chang, H., Ngunjiri, F. W., & Hernandez, K. A. C. (2012). *Collaborative Autoethnography* (Vol. 8). Walnut Creek: Left Coast Press.

Chinn, P. W. U. (1995). *Becoming A Scientist: Narratives of Women Entering Science and Engineering*. Ed.D. Thesis. University of Hawaii. Ann Arbor: UMI Dissertation Services.

Clifford, G. J. (1989). *Lone Voyagers: Academic Women in Coeducational Universities, 1870–1937*. New York: Feminist Press at CUNY.

Clifford, G. (2014). *Those Good Gertrudes: A Social History of Women Teachers in America*. Baltimore, MD: Johns Hopkins University Press.

Cole, A. L., & Knowles, G. J. (2001). *Lives in Context: The Art of Life History Research*. Lanham, MD: AltaMira Press.

Connors, R. (1992). Dreams and play: Historical method and methodology. In G. Kirsch & P. A. Sullivan (Eds.), *Methods and Methodology in Composition Research* (pp. 15–36). Carbondale, IL: Southern Illinois UP.

Creswell, J. W. (2013). *Qualitative Inquiry and Research Design: Choosing Among Five Approaches*. Thousand Oaks: Sage.

Davies, B. (2006). *Doing Collective Biography: Investigating the Production of Subjectivity*. New York: Open University Press.

Davies, B., & Gannon, S. (2006). *Doing Collective Biography: Investigating the Production of Subjectivity*. Open University Press.

Denzin, N. (2006). Analytic autoethnography, or deja vu all over again. *Journal of Contemporary Ethnography*, *35*, 419–428.

Denzin, N., & Lincoln, Y., Eds. (2005). *Handbook of Qualitative Research* (3rd ed.). Thousand Oaks: Sage.

Dollard, J. (1935/1949). *Criteria for the Life History, With Analysis of Six Notable Documents*. New York: Peter Smith.

Edel, L. (1984). Transference: The biographer's dilemma. *Biography*, 7(4), 283–291.

Edward Sapir, E. (1932). Cultural anthropology and psychiatry. *Journal of Abnormal and Social Psychology*, *27*, 229–242.

Elk, B. (1932). *Black Elk Speaks: Being the Life Story of a Holy Man of the Oglala Sioux*. Lincoln, NE: University of Nebraska Press.

Ellis, C. (2004). *The Ethnographic I: A Methodological Novel about Teaching and Doing Autoethnography*. Walnut Creek: Alta Mira.

Ellis, C., Adams, T. E., & Bochner, A. P. (2010). Autoethnography: An overview [40 paragraphs]. *Forum Qualitative Sozialforschung/Forum: Qualitative Social Research*, *12*(1), Art. 10, http://nbn-resolving.de/urn:nbn:de:0114-fqs1101108

Ellis, C., & Bochner, A. P. (2000). Autoethnography, personal narrative, reflexivity. In N. K. Denzin & Y. S. Lincoln (Eds.), *Handbook of Qualitative Research* (2nd ed., pp. 733–768). Thousand Oaks, CA: Sage.

Ellis, C., & Bochner, A. P. (2006). Analyzing analytic autoethnography: An autopsy. *Journal of Contemporary Ethnography, 35*(4), 429–449.

Erard, C., & Bancel, N. (2007). Prosopographical analysis of sports elites: Overview and evaluation of a seminal study. *The International Journal of the History of Sport, 24*(1), 67–79.

Fairclough, N. (2001). *Language and Power*. New York: Pearson Education.

Ferrarotti, F. (1983). Biography and the social sciences. *Social Research, 50*(1), 57–80.

Frank, G. (1979). Finding the common denominator: A phenomenological critique of life history method. *Ethos, 7*(1), 68–94.

Garbati, J., & Rothschild, N. (2016). Lasting impact of study abroad experiences: A collaborative autoethnography. *Forum Qualitative Sozialforschung / Forum: Qualitative Social Research, 17*(2). Retrieved from www.qualitative-research.net/index.php/fqs/article/view/2387

Geertz, C. (1994). Thick description: Toward an interpretive theory of culture. In M. Martin & L. C. McIntyre (Eds.), *Readings in the Philosophy of Social Science* (pp. 213–231). Boston, MA: MIT Press.

Gonick, M., Walsh, S., & Brown, M. (2011). Collective biography and the question of difference. *Qualitative Inquiry, 17*(8), 741–749.

Gordon, M. (1996). *The Shadow Man: A Daughter's Search for Her Father*. New York: Random.

Hatch, A. J., & Wisniewski, R. (1995). Life history and narrative: Questions, issues and exemplary works. In J. A. Hatch & R. Wisniewski (Eds.), *Life History and Narrative* (pp. 113–136). Washington, DC: Falmer.

Haug, F. (1987). *Female Sexualization: A Collective Work of Memory* (Vol. 25). London: Verso.

Hawkins, R., Al-Hindi, K. F., Moss, P., & Kern, L. (2016). Practicing collective biography. *Geography Compass, 10*(4), 165–178.

Holman Jones, S., Adams, T., & Ellis, C. (2013). *Handbook of Autoethnography*. Walnut Creek, CA: Left Coast Press.

Holt, N. L. (2003). Representation, legitimation, and autoethnography: An autoethnographic writing story. *International Journal of Qualitative Methods, 2*(1), 18–28.

Hudson, L. M. (2009). Lies, secrets, and silences: Writing African American women's biography. *Journal of Women's History, 21*(4), 138–140.

Hughes, S., Pennington, J. L., & Makris, S. (2012). Translating autoethnography across the AERA standards toward understanding autoethnographic scholarship as empirical research. *Educational Researcher, 41*(6), 209–219.

Janesick, V. J. (2007). Oral history as a social justice project: Issues for the qualitative researcher. *The Qualitative Report, 12*(1), 111–121. Retrieved from www.nova.edu/ssss/QR/QR12-1/janesick.pdf

Janesick, V. J. (2010). *Oral History for the Qualitative Researcher: Choreographing the Story*. New York: Guilford Press.

Jenkinson, J. (1993). *Scottish Medical Societies, 1731–1939: Their History and Records.* Edinburgh: Edinburgh University Press.

Jenkinson, J. (2016). Administering relief: Glasgow Corporation's support for Scotland's c. 20,000 Belgian refugees 1. *Immigrants and Minorities, 34*(2), 171–191.

Jones, S. H. (2016). Living bodies of thought: The "critical" in critical ethnography. *Qualitative Inquiry, 22*(4), 228–237.

Kelly, H. (2013). Toward a critical race biography of Marion Thompson Wright (1905–1962): Finding facts, pivoting race. *Vitae Schloasticae: The Journal of Educational Biography, 30*(2), 43–65.

Kern, L., Hawkins, R., Al-Hindi, K. F., & Moss, P. (2014). A collective biography of joy in academic practice. *Social and Cultural Geography, 15*(7), 834–851.

Kohli, M. (1981). Biography: Account, text, method. In D. Bertaux (Ed.), *Biography and Society: The Life History Approach to Social Sciences* (pp. 61–75). London: Sage.

Kouritzin, S. G. (2000). Bringing life to research: Life history research and ESL. *TESL Canada Journal, 17*(2), 35.

Kridel, C., Ed. (1998). *Writing Educational Biography.* New York: Garland/Routledge.

Leiris, M. (1946). L'Âge d'homme. Paris: Gallimard.

Leggo, C. (2004). Light and shadow: Four reasons for writing (and not writing) autobiographically. *Vitae Scholasticae: The Journal of Educational Biography, 21*(1), 5–22.

Leggo, C. (2005). Autobiography and identity: Six speculations. *Vitae Scholasticae: The Journal of Educational Biography, 22*(1), 115–133.

Lieblich, A. (2004). Writing biography as a relationship. *Nashim: A Journal of Jewish Women's Studies and Gender Issues, 7*(1), 206–211.

Lightfoot, S. L. (1988). *Balm in Gilead: Journey of a Healer.* New York: Random House.

Long, J. (1999). *Telling Women's Lives: Subject/Narrator/Reader/Text.* New York: New York University Press.

Magdalino, P. (2003). 'Prosopography and Byzantine identity' in Fifty Years of Prosopography. In A. Cameron (Ed.), *Proceedings of the British Academy* (pp. 41–56). Oxford, UK: Oxford University Press.

Martin, J. (2005). Gender, the city and the politics of schooling: towards a collective biography of women 'doing good' as public moralists in Victorian London. *Gender and Education, 17*(2), 143–163.

McHugh, S. (2007). The aerobic art of interviewing. *Asia Pacific Media Educator, 18*, 147–154.

McKee, H. A., & Porter, J. E. (2012). The ethics of archival research. *College Composition and Communication, 64*(1), 59–81.

Measor, L., & Sikes, P. (1992). Visiting lives: Ethics and methodology in life history. In I. F. Goodson (Ed.), *Studying Teachers Lives* (pp. 209–233). New York: Teachers College Press.

Merrill, B., & West, L. (2009). *Using Biographical Methods in Social Research*. Thousand Oaks: Sage.

Mills, C. W. (1959). *The Sociological Imagination*. Oxford: Oxford University Press.

Minge, J. M. (2013). Mindful autoethnography, local knowledges. In S. Holman Jones, T. E. Adams, & C. Ellis (Eds.), *Handbook of Autoethnography* (pp. 425–442). Walnut Creek, CA: Left Coast Press.

Morgan, A. (2013). *A Collective Biography of the Founders of the American Association of University Women*. Unpublished doctoral dissertation, Ball State University (USA).

Mulvihill, T. (1999). Hart to Hart: Sisters working in tandem for educational change in nineteenth century America. *Vitae Scholasticae: The Bulletin of Educational Biography, 18*(1) (Caddo Gap Press), 79–95.

Mulvihill, T. (2000). Sarton May I? Using the life and work of May Sarton as a pedagogical tool. *Vitae Scholasticae: The Bulletin of Educational Biography, 18*(2) [Fall 1999 (Caddo Gap Press, arrived in print Spring, 2000)], 95–106.

Mulvihill, T. (Autumn, 2009). The universal declaration of human rights and education: Examining the issues and vital voices for women and girls through comparative educational biography. *Hudson Valley Review, 26*(1), 53–67.

Mulvihill, T. M., & Latz, A. O. (2011). Choreographing intertextual stories: Qualitative inquiry meets oral history. *The Qualitative Report, 16*(3), 892–896.

Neale, B., & Bishop, L. (2012). The Timescapes Archive: A stakeholder approach to archiving qualitative longitudinal data. *Qualitative Research, 12*(1), 53–65.

Noblit, G. W., & Hare, R. D. (1988). *Meta-Ethnography: Synthesizing Qualitative Studies* (Vol. 11). Thousand Oaks: Sage.

Oates, S. B., Ed. (1986). *Biography as High Adventure: Life-Writers Speak on Their Art*. Amherst: University of Massachusetts Press.

Oates, S. (1991). *Biography as History*. Mankham Press Fund. Waco, TX: Baylor University Press.

Oldfield, S.-J. (2015). Narrative methods in sport history research: Biography, collective biography, and prosopography. *The International Journal of the History of Sport, 32*(15), 1855–1882.

Paulette, L. (1993). A choice for K'aila. *Humane Medicine, 9*(1), 13–17.

Perks, R., & Thomson, A. (2006). Introduction to second edition. *The Oral History Reader* (2nd ed., pp. ix–xiv). London: Routledge.

Peters, M. (1981). Group biography: Challenges and methods. In A. M. Friedson (Ed.), *New Directions in Biography* (pp. 41–51). Honolulu: Biographical Research Center.

Plummer, K. (2001). The call of life stories in ethnographic research. In P. Atkinson, A. Coffey, S. Delamont, J. Lofland, & L. Lofland (Eds.), *Handbook of Ethnography* (pp. 395–406). London: Sage.

Portelli, A. (1997). *The Battle of Valle Giulia: Oral History and the Art of Dialogue*. Madison: University of Wisconsin Press.

Radin, P., Ed. (1926). *Crashing Thunder: The Autobiography of an American Indian*. New York and London: Appleton and Co.

Riessman, C. K. (2003). Performing identities in illness narrative: Masculinity and multiple sclerosis. *Qualitative Research, 3*(1), 5–33.

Ritchie, J., Spencer, L., & O'Connor, W. (2003). Carrying out qualitative analysis. In J. Ritchie & J. Lewis (Eds.), *Qualitative Research Practice: A Guide for Social Science Students and Researchers* (pp. 219–262). London: Sage.

Sage, L. (2000). *Bad Blood*. London: Fourth Estate.

Saldana, J. (2013). *The Coding Manual for Qualitative Researchers*. (2nd ed.). London: Sage.

Sarton, M. (1973). *Journal of a Solitude*. New York: W.W. Norton & Company.

Sawyer, R. D., & Norris, J. (2013). *Duoethnography: Understanding Qualitative Research*. New York: Oxford University Press.

Schutze, F. (1983). Biographical research and narrative interview. *Neue Praxis, 13*, 283–293.

Shopes, L. (2011). Oral history. In N. K. Denzin & Y. S. Lincoln (Eds.), *The SAGE Handbook of Qualitative Research*. Thousand Oaks: Sage.

Shostack, M. (1981). *Nisa: The Life and Words of a !Kung Woman*. Cambridge: Harvard University Press.

Smith, L. M. (2012). Nora Barlow: A tale of a Darwin granddaughter. *Vitae Scholasticae, 29*(2), 58–76.

Smith, L. M. (2014). Adventuring as biographers: A chronicle of a difficult ten-day week. *Vitae Scholasticae, 31*(1), 5–22.

Smith, S. (1987). The impact of critical theory on the study of autobiography: Marginality, gender, and autobiographical practice. *Auto/Biography Studies, 3*(3), 1–12.

Smith, S., & Watson, J. (2010). *Reading Autobiography: A Guide for Interpreting Life Narratives*. Minneapolis, MN: University of Minnesota Press.

Sparkes, A. C. (2000). Autoethnography and narratives of self: Reflections on criteria in action. *Sociology of Sport Journal, 17*(1), 21–43.

Spry, T. (2001). Performing autoethnography: An embodied methodological praxis. *Qualitative Inquiry, 7*(6), 706–732.

Spry, T. (2011). *Body, Paper, Stage: Writing and Performing Autoethnography*. Walnut Creek: Left Coast Press.

Stanley, L. (1992). *The Auto/biographical*. Manchester, UK: Manchester University Press.

Stanley, L. (1993). On auto/biography in sociology. *Sociology, 27*(1), 41–52.

Szczepanik, R., & Siebert, S. (2015). The triple bind of narration: Fritz Schüt-ze's biographical interview in prison research and beyond. *Sociology, 50*(2), 285–300.

Tedlock, B. (2013). Braiding evocative with analytic autoethnography. In S. Holman Jones, T. E. Adams, & C. Ellis (Eds.), *Handbook of Autoethnography* (pp. 368–362). Walnut Creek, CA: Left Coast Press.

Terkel, S., Ed. (1974). *Working: People Talk About What They Do All Day and How They Feel About What They Do.* New York: The New Press.

Tesar, M. (2015). Ethics and truth in archival research. *History of Education, 44*(1), 101–114.

Thomas, W. I., & Znaniecki, F. (1918). *The Polish Peasant in Europe and America: Monograph of an Immigrant Group* (Vol. 2). Chicago, IL: University of Chicago Press.

Tillman, L. M. (2013). Wedding album. In S. Holman Jones, T. E. Adams, & C. Ellis (Eds.), *Handbook of Autoethnography* (pp. 478–485). Walnut Creek, CA: Left Coast Press.

Urban, W. J., Ed. (2012). *Leaders in the Historical Study of American Education* (Vol. 3). New York: Springer Science & Business Media.

Watson, L. C., & Watson-Franke, M. B. (1985). *Interpreting Life Histories: An Anthropological Inquiry.* New Brunswick, NJ: Rutgers University Press.

Weiner, G. (2008). Olive Banks and the collective biography of British feminism. *British Journal of Sociology of Education, 29*(4), 403–410.

Wheeler, S. (2004). Polar gap. In M. Bostridge (Ed.), *Lives for Sale: Biographer's Tales* (pp. 86–89). London: Bloomsbury Academic Press.

Wolcott, H. F. (2009). *Writing Up Qualitative Research* (3rd ed.). Thousand Oaks: Sage.

Wolff, G. (1979). Minor lives. In M. Pachter (Ed.), *Telling Lives: The Biographer's Art.* Washington, DC: New Republic Books, 56–72.

Woolf, V. (1985). *Moments of Being.* Boston, MA: Houghton Mifflin Harcourt.

3

PRACTICAL APPLICATIONS AND DREAMSCAPES FOR LIFE WRITERS

Themes that will comprise this chapter include the relationship between the life writer and the subject; an example of a life writing project exploring the role eulogy or memorialization plays in how some narrate a life; the treatment of voice in life writing; and the lived experience and identity of the life writer. This chapter will also address the issues related to navigating the use of public and private archives, curating and building open-sourced secondary data collections, encouraging the multimodal nature of visual and interactive life writing spaces, and the bridges to theatrical performances related to life writing collaborations. And finally, the metaphor of a dreamscape will be used to illustrate the life writers' spirit of adventure and excitement in attempting to narrate a life that will always remain a partial mystery and grapples with the various epistemologies that can frame such projects. Dreamscapes allow for "practical dreaming," a way by which life writers can use their imagination, positionality, and critical reflexivity tools to engage with their projects.

Critical Reflexivity

Critical reflexivity is at the heart of all qualitative inquiry projects, including life writing.

"Reflexivity is commonly viewed as the process of a continual internal dialogue and critical self-evaluation of a researcher's positionality as well as active acknowledgement and explicit recognition that this position may affect the research process" (Berger, 2015, p. 220). The methodological literature has many examples of engaging reflexively with research projects. For example, Cunliffe (2004) offers ways to engage in critically reflexive practice including examples of "critically reflexive journaling" (p. 407). And Swaminathan and Mulvihill (2017) look at how qualitative researchers build and use critical questions at all stages of a study. These practical applications of critical reflexivity will help guide life writing projects even at the stage where you are considering what type of project to pursue.

The Process of Selecting a Life Writing Project

What is the start of the journey of life writing? It is hard at times to pinpoint that exact moment or the questions that provoked the start of a long research and travel with a person or people whom one will get to know intimately over time. Claire Tomalin, who wrote the biography of Hardy, explained how she became interested in the subject. In an email communication to Leader (2015), she said of Hardy, "I believed him when he said he was a poet who turned to fiction to earn his living, and it seemed worth taking this seriously" (p. 6). Many times there are moments when, as life writers who want to learn more, we have a question or a concern that we want to answer or verify. In doing so, it leads to a longer journey where we learn from our subjects and in many cases they tend to become our companions. Forster (2004) explained that a series of coincidences convinced her that it was, in fact, her subject, Daphne Du Maurier, that chose her even though she had neither met her nor corresponded with her. She described how the book *Rebecca* falls on her from a bookshelf, her own excitement at finding in this way a subject for a biography just as she was seeking one, her correspondence with her agent, and subsequent proposal to the estate of Du Maurier to write an official biography. These backstories about how life writers become engaged with their projects are informative and often very intriguing.

Perhaps it is a theme that moves us to find out more. Life writing need not be confined to an intense focus on one person; it can take on a broader challenge. The life writing impulse can be ignited by a question that needs to be answered through examples drawn from several lives. For example, Hermione Lee (2015), an accomplished literary biographer, has examined encounters between people in the limelight. She drew on memoirs and biographies to describe the multiple and varied descriptions of meetings that she refers to as "literary encounters." She examined encounters between musicians (Puccini and Schoenberg), between artists (Walt Disney and Stravinsky regarding Fantasia), and writers (Oscar Wilde and Walt Whitman). In each description, she discussed the role of memory, giving credence to the theory of memory as explicated by Bartlett (1932) that memory is reconstructive as opposed to reproductive. In retelling stories from memory or in describing encounters, the telling and retelling of a story is more a reconstruction of the event rather than a faithful reproduction, as each of the people involved may tell the story differently and rival versions may emerge as a result.

Comparative Educational Biography Project Example

This next section provides an example of how a comparative educational biography project, exploring the role of eulogy and memorialization, is outlined methodologically and how two life writers collaborate.

Theoretical Perspective

We framed this methodological exploration using a constructionist epistemology (Crotty, 1998) using narrative theory approaches (Creswell, 2013), which informed our interpretive (biographical) theoretical perspective (Denzin, 1989; Kridel, 1998). Data sources come from two educational biography projects and were used to illustrate the following methodological issues: a.) relationship between auto/biographer and subject, b.) critique of eulogy/memorialization auto/biographies, and c.) the effects of collaboration on constructing critical auto/biographies.

Project one (Mulvihill) examined the educational biography of a Waldorf education student who died in a car accident at the age of 10 as she was being driven to school by her teenage brother, also a member of the school, and the response of the educational community that used biography and autobiography to grieve, create meaning, and heal. Data sources included semi-structured interviews with key participants, artifacts such as artwork created by children in the school, performance-ethnography pieces related to eurhythmy (a form of storytelling through dance and body movement originated by Rudolf Steiner and Marie von Sivers, associated with the Theosophical Society of the early twentieth century), fieldnotes generated from the educational biographer's participant-observation experiences, and secondary sources found by way of a focused literature review about Waldorf education and the uses of auto/biography in the Waldorf curriculum, as well as the methodological literature related to critical auto/biography, including the use of qualitative inquiry tools to shape the project.

Project two (Swaminathan) examined the educational biographies of Annie Besant and Krishnamurti. Both Annie Besant and Krishnamurti played important and significant roles in the educational life of India. Several biographies and autobiographies have been written about and by Annie Besant, who actively participated in India's political and social life by founding schools and colleges and, in addition, participated in India's Independence movement. Krishnamurti, adopted by Annie Besant as a young boy, was brought up to be a world teacher within the Theosophical Society movement. As an adult he declared that he was not a world teacher and departed from the Theosophical Society and went on to found several schools in India, England, and the United States and Canada, the majority of which are active and considered successful holistic schools. Data sources for this project included Annie Besant and Krishnamurti's writings on education, their autobiographical writings, their journals, as well as biographies of their lives. Biographical writings are examined for their contributions, omissions, invisibilities, or overt explanations regarding decisions made by Annie Besant and Krishnamurti in their lives. Recently released journal writings of Krishnamurti's close associates that detail the everyday life of Krishnamurti also inform this project. The approach to this biographical project is informed by the work of Amia Lieblich

(2004), who explains that writing biography is both a study and a relationship, and by feminist writers such as Carolyn Heilbrun (1988). In this sense, it is a relational project wherein an overt acknowledgement of the biographer's own connections to Krishnamurti the person and his philosophy of education are integral to the narrative.

These examples explored the different ways in which critical auto/biographical methods can enhance/elevate life writing projects by examining eulogy/memorialization narratives, and the analysis resulted in meaningful methodological insights. The following methodological themes resulted from this critical auto/biographical investigation and were identified as part of this collaborative analytical dialogic process between two auto/biographers working on intersecting projects: (1) the relationship between the auto/biographer and the subject; (2) the critique of eulogy or memorialization auto/biographies using a critical theory lens; (3) various treatments of voice and narration in critical auto/biography; and (4) the role of the researcher (auto/biographer) identity in such projects.

Eulogy and memorialization studies of events, people, and places in the projects that we have outlined from a critical lens serve to remind us that biographies/autobiographies are necessarily incomplete. They teach us to look for and examine omissions and ask questions such as whom does this auto/biography serve or for what purpose is it written? Although memorialization and eulogy studies are overtly subjective, the questions that serve biography projects are questions regarding the emotions or subjective relationship between the biographer and the subject. For example, the biography of Annie Besant by Ann Taylor (1992) is a case in point of a lack of empathy or relationship between the biographer and subject. Other studies, for example the biographies by Mary Lutyens of Krishnamurti, leave out important details of his personal life that were brought up in later biographies and created considerable stir among those who admired Krishnamurti and his teachings. In the case of how Waldorf schools position biographies and autobiographies as therapeutic storytelling in moments of profound grief, critical auto/biography perspectives can be useful to help illuminate the various ways grief and healing are culturally constructed and to what degree members of this Waldorf educational community adhere to the a/r/tography of constructing eulogy narratives.

The resulting claims, evidence, and warrants from the two projects led us to conclude that examining eulogy/memorialization auto/biographies helps us to interrogate and inform critical auto/biography methods. In conclusion, a close examination of innovative approaches used in narrating critical auto/biographies provided the authors with new methodological tools.

The significance of this study is situated within the methodological insights generated when two auto/biographers collaboratively examined eulogy/memorialization narratives through the lens of critical auto/biography and assembled an analysis that created potential new pathways for critical life writers working in collaboration. Shortland and Yeo (2008) pointed out that as "every age defines itself, new questions come to be asked of biography" (p. 2). Perhaps the corollary ought to be, as new questions come to be asked of the rhizomatic nature (Stehlik, 2004; Irwin, Beer, Springgay, Grauer, Xiong, and Bickel, 2006; Collier, Moffatt, and Perry, 2015) of the genre we call critical auto/biography, so, too, new questions ought to be asked about critical auto/biographers themselves and the methodological moves they make as they more fully understand the rhizomatic nature of life writing. This process, in essence, is a shift of epistemological beliefs. And, as Gunn reminds us, auto/biography is not the "private act of self-writing" but the "cultural act of self-reading" (p. 8). Through our projects and work on critical life writing methods, we have learned to engage in a reflexive and "disciplined subjectivity" (Shortland and Yeo, 2008, p. 34) whereby the relationship between the biographer and subject is interrogated and a new "wide-awakeness" (Greene, 1977; 1978) results within these life writing collaborations. And, we suggest that, where possible and appropriate, new collaborative efforts between life writers across related projects will further accentuate the rhizomatic nature of this form of life writing and elevate critical life writing into new innovative shapes.

Collaborative Life Writing: Issues of Power in Life Writing

Collaborative life writing examples include celebrity memoirs that are ghost written and ethnographic autobiographies. Both are writings where the subject narrates the story to the writer. Issues of power in both cases need to be attended to; as in celebrity collective life writing, the subject exceeds the writer in power while the opposite is often the case in ethnographic life writing. The final book or manuscript often excludes the intervening process, the interviews, and the voice of the writer, ensuring that the end product resembles one writer rather than a collective effort. In the *Autobiography of Malcolm X*, Alex Haley writes an epilogue that makes the process visible. He explains the devices he used in order to persuade Malcolm X to talk openly and, further, discusses the times when the collaboration was filled with tension.

Power in life writing is particularly problematic and needs to be examined when dealing with the issue of rapport. While all qualitative research methods urge researchers to create a rapport with the participant, it is important to think about and exercise reflexivity with regard to the potentially dangerous and exploitative aspect of rapport building. It is possible to exploit rapport for research purposes and at times it can confirm or validate a deviant identity. In some situations, it is possible for the researcher to feel discomfort while generating rapport while, at the same time, it can also be exploitative on the part of the researcher. Gary Fine (1987) while conducting participant observation with Little League baseball players, found himself several times in situations where he had to decide whether or not to intervene as an "adult" in a child's world, risk foregoing any rapport advantage or any further access to group behavior that they might cover up in the presence of an adult authority figure. Fine (1987) discussed his role and the ethical issues he faced and the justifications that he made, including the justification of not interfering with the scientific nature of the research and allowing events to unfold without interfering. Ultimately, the life writer will have to make clear-eyed decisions that can be defended, and becoming familiar with the various ways other life writers have reasoned through their own decisions can be instructive.

Treatment of Voice in Life Writing

As in all writing projects, the concept of voice and the decisions qualitative inquiry researchers need to address when crafting narrations are deserving of deep and careful thinking.

What is the voice we should use in life writing? Should our voices focus on the inner self and, if so, how does one integrate personal experiences with the questions we might want to explore? The focus on the self in life writing genres (e.g., autoethnography) has also led to debates around the voice of the narrator. Tierney (2002) raises questions about the "unreflexive insertion of the author into a narrative" (p. 8). He raises concerns resulting from the crisis of representation that arose from the criticism of positivist narratives. While Tierney (2002) equally critiques research where the author is absent or adopts the perspective of an omniscient self, he also critiques what he describes as an uncritical adoption of the personal narrative by qualitative researchers in general and unreflexive autoethnographers in particular. He points out that the voice of the narrator is crucial in a story and that writers need to reflect on how the narrator's voice fits with the story s/he wants to tell in addition to reflecting on facets of storytelling, such as the use of time in narrative. He calls for a greater diversity of ways in which the author's narrative voice might come into play in a story. He cautions that such diversity of representation should not result in a sole focus on the autobiographical self at the expense of a concern to understand the lives of the "other." In this sense he advocates for life writers to continue to work on "other focused" ethnographic narratives. In a response to Ellis (2002), Tierney (2002) outlined the critical differences between the two scholars. If Tierney saw autoethnography as a movement away from the other, Ellis saw autoethnography firmly embedded in the other involving "critical engagement, social problems and social action" (p. 401). Tracing these evolving understandings and intellectual debates within the literature provide an important window into the contours of the dilemmas life writers face and ultimately what impact that thinking has on the shape of a project.

Amia Lieblich (2004) discusses her struggle to find the right voice in her biographical projects. As a feminist scholar, a woman writing about women, she found examples of biographies that aimed to blend history with literary style limiting as she sat in her room, wondering about the multiple narratives about her subject, Dvora Baron, that warred in her head. Feeling stuck, she had an epiphany that freed her up to write and find her voice. She invited a conversation with

Dvora Baron, and although Baron had died in 1956 and the year Lieblich was writing was 1990, she nevertheless found her voice through a series of conversations with her subject. Through these conversations, she discussed many topics including her public life, her later withdrawal from the same, her relationship with her daughter, and her health. Through these conversations, Lieblich approached biography as a relational project. She critiques the stance of the "neutral biographer" as she asks whether it is possible for biographers to be emotionally distant from their subjects. She points out that the biographer's attachment and sentiments, whether they be positive or negative, have usually been kept out of the biographies themselves, reflecting what she refers to as "men's ways of knowing" as opposed to "women's ways of knowing" (Belenky, Clinchy, Goldberger, and Tarule, 1997). In Lieblich's (2004) view, the "art of biography-writing, then, is, that of constructing a relationship, of being inside a dialogue while constantly reflecting upon it" (p. 209). In terms of the voice of the biographer, she believes that the biography needs to find a way to allow the voice of the subject to emerge while the biographer serves as a witness and as a listener and responder to the life she is studying.

Nadel (1984) identifies three approaches or narrative stances that can be identified in the genre of biography: dramatic/expressive, objective/academic, and the interpretive/analytic. To what extent the biographer can insert themselves into the story has been a subject of debate in the genre. On the one hand, Garrison (1992) writes, "the biographer must contend with the impulse to tell one's own life story in the process of writing someone else's." On the other hand, Geoffrey Wolff (1979) points out that "to deny biography the signature of a style, the sound of a single voice rather than a crow-noise of the species Biographer, seems perverse, artless, and servile."

Biographers often describe their own connection with their subjects, even if that connection is forged during the process of writing and researching the lives of their subjects. Forster (2004) refers to her connections with Du Maurier in different ways. She refers to their common distaste for publicity and shopping. She explains how difficult it was for her to have to appear at events to promote her biography but thought it important to be with her subject and stand by what she wrote. As she put it, she hated "all publicity (just as Daphne did)" and "again like Daphne . . . loathe[d] shopping" (p. 56). Unlike Forster, Robb (2004) discusses his biographical relationship with his subject as detached but not devoid of emotion. Regarding it as an advantage, he says that if a biographer has a loving relationship with the subject, there is a danger that the biographer may misrepresent or omit details that cast their subject in an unfavorable light. Writing biography comprises two narrative strands coming together—the narrative of the subject and the narrative of the biographer coming to know, structure, and recreate the life of the subject. This process can lead the researcher through a process where the biographer can come to know and admire or reject with disgust their subjects or identify strongly with them. Emotions are part of the getting to know the subject process in writing biography. Backscheider (1999) describes the process as one where the biographer is both a friend and an enemy of the subject: "The biographer becomes the subject's closest ally and bitterest enemy. All biographers must be their subjects' advocates, taking up the burden of explaining lives and why they were led as they were." The narrative of biography, therefore, describes the emotional map of the biographer, where the researcher liked and loved the subject, and where the researcher was sympathetic and where the biography laid bare acts that were repugnant or baffling to the researcher. A second, parallel narrative that one finds in biography is the narrative of place, where the biographer travels to find the documents, the letters, the photographs, the fragments that, taken together, form a more complex if not whole picture. This narrative is one of the activities the biographer undertakes, the interviews she conducts, and the places she visits to recapture the life of the subject. Hibbard (2006) refers to this relationship as the "dialectical relationship between biographer and subject."

Treatment of Agency in Life Writing

Finding the right voice is intimately related to figuring out strategies for agency in life writing. How can life writers either reproduce or resist popular and stereotypical ways in which cultural stories have scripted them as particular subjects? Finding ways to disrupt the cultural scripts means finding strategies that will emancipate the life writer. For Hilary Mantel (2003), life writing was a way to "seize the copyright in myself" (p. 81). Suffering from illnesses and pain, her body is constantly labeled, misdiagnosed as she writes of the humiliation of being regarded as neurotic or "little miss neverwell" (p. 82). Life writing became a way to assert agency, to recover her sense of self as she wrote her story that included the parts of a life she could not live. She uses life writing as a way to recover and create a coherent self from the array of labels that the medical establishment used to refer to her body and self.

Dreamscapes

The metaphor of a dreamscape can be used to illustrate the life writers' spirit of adventure and excitement in attempting to narrate a life that will always remain a partial mystery and grapples with the various epistemologies that can frame such projects. Dreamscapes allow for "practical dreaming," a way by which life writers can use their imagination, positionality, and critical reflexivity tools to engage with their projects (Mulvihill and Swaminathan, 2012).

Challenges and Opportunities Faced by Life Writers

Besides limitations of memory and issues that surround the actual search for facets of a life, life writer researchers face the challenge of having enough to say about all phases of a life. If the objective is to write a life, and if the main events or highlights occur during a particular phase, the question of how to write up the life instead of wondering what to say about the intervening years between significant events is a challenge not easily resolved in life writing. This is also the challenge of not having enough resources to draw upon. As Wheeler (2004) queries, "How is one to fill the gaps? You can't make it up; you can't invite the reader to take his choice; you can't do anything" (p. 88). The biographer tries to create an organized life out of what sources are available, and yet as Wheeler (2004) says, she tries to resist this desire to "impose coherence (seeing so clearly that in my own life there is none)" (p. 88). How is a life writer to make sense of the past and to recreate it? Or rather how is a life writer to take the outward facts that are available and yet find a way to create the inner life, the emotions and habits that make it complex and yet whole? The attempt to craft a life out of the pieces of evidence available is much like trying to pin down the human spirit—our narrative often runs up against neat categorizations. Wheeler (2004) says that "biographies tend to fail if they take a doggedly factual approach that ignores the gloopy layers of emotional and imaginative experience that make us human" (p. 88).

How can a biographer avoid feeling like a voyeur when confronted with sources and tales or evidence that one knows the subject tried to conceal during her lifetime? Biographers and life writers also confront the issue of obtaining permissions for items in archives. Confidentiality clauses governing "personality rights" need to be examined and the tedious task of writing for permissions has to be endured.

Life Writing in the Digital Era: Challenges and Opportunities

Researchers in the field of life writing have begun to question what sources they can turn to in the digital era where the familiar paper diaries, documents, letters, and notebooks are absent or converting into digital reproductions. How can a researcher approach life writing and what methodological approaches are available or appropriate?

Life writing in the digital era offers up new spaces in the public and private sphere for researchers to explore in blogs, personal web pages, and video or audio recordings. Would the individual remain the central point of reference in the digital age where links are many and the network is structurally embedded in such writing and recording? As Heinrich and Soeting (2015) ask, what would be the status of the subject in a "culture that increasingly regards the network rather than the individual as its central point of reference" (p. i)? Arthur likens smartphones and other portable electronic devices as "biography machines" (Arthur, 2014).

Methodological Tools in Life Writing: Advantages and Limitations

Life-Grids

While biographical interviewing is a robust method that yields dense data, there is no doubt that interviewing is also time consuming. When biographical projects need to be completed within a short time frame or are less focused on the particular individual's life story and more on a comparative analysis of experiences across several life stories, life-grids may be one way to gather biographical data. Life-grids can precede an interview and can be used to collect biographical data that can be analyzed easily across cases.

For a successful qualitative life-grid design, decisions regarding what the life-grid will represent need to be made. Themes are usually placed across the top of the grid and may include key events in the life history of the participants. For example, some themes that might garner useful information may be family, education, health, housing, partners, or jobs. On the left side of the grid, time spans are marked. Time spans may be marked on the basis of particular milestones depending on the project. Abbas, Ashwin, and Maclean (2015) used life-grids for a study that analyzed the validity of the league table representations of four university sociology departments by examining the experiences and transformations of students at these institutions. For their study, time spans were based on the milestones of the educational system.

Life-grids may at times serve to put participants at ease since filling out the grid is a collaborative effort on the part of the researcher and the participant. It may allow researchers to be more sensitive when tailoring interviews to individuals. The form of the life-grid or its design can have an effect on the type of data gathered, as a pre-imposed structure might constrain some participants from expressing themselves freely. In addition, since lives do not fit into neat boxes, the question of what to do with or how to approach those participants who may want to go outside the box remains. To prevent over-determining what participants have to offer, researchers have to use life-grids with sensitivity and move to other forms of data gathering, including taking notes if participants wish to blur the boxes of the life-grid.

Life Lines

A related tool are life lines, which can be used with semi-structured interview methods as ways to elicit deeper conversation about "highs and lows" within a life, or "most memorable moments" whereby the person is asked not to list out life events but rather to immediately assign some value to "most meaningful" and for what reasons. Life lines focus on key incidents, significant emotional moments, periods where disorienting dilemmas were present, etc. Asking a person to narrate their life using a life lines approach often produces juxtapositions that open up new lines of dialogue and insight.

Life History Calendar Method

Freedman, Thornton, and Camburn (1988) outlined a life history calendar method for gathering data. The life history calendar is a tool used to gather retrospective data. It is regarded as a way to improve recall of past events, especially if several events unfolded at similar times. It is also regarded as an advantage in remembering detailed sequences of events. The life history calendar is a document that gathers together in one place all the different event histories that a researcher is intent on gathering. The time units in such a calendar are determined by the type of data required. Some researchers incorporate the calendar or grid into a survey questionnaire. This tool can, at a glance, record births, marriages, work, migration, specific exchanges—for example, money interchange between parents and children. The time unit can therefore be a day, week, or a month depending on how often the activity is likely to occur. While this tool has been used to gather retrospective data from several respondents, our suggestion would be to use this tool in conjunction with life history interviews.

Imagined Dialogues

Imagined dialogues can be a tool for life writers as well as for analyzing life writing. It can serve as a way for the researcher to interact with the person whose life is being examined; it can be used as a tool to examine an altered point of view between the author and the different people with whom one interacts. Imagined dialogues may also be used as an analytical tool for life writers to get at different points of view. Imagined dialogues can take the form of letters, diaries, and imagined conversations to bridge the gaps between what is known about the subject and what remains as questions (Mulvihill, Swaminathan, and Bailey, 2015).

Research Journal and Sketchbook Exercise 17

Write an analytical memo representing an imagined dialogue between two people, and then write about how this exercise may have opened up the possibilities for more nuanced questions you might entertain as part of a life writing project.

Obituaries

Obituaries offer opportunities to examine many things:

1. The cultural and historical assumptions about a life course
2. Cultural conventions about record keeping
3. Narrative strategies used to communicate the end of a life
4. What is highlighted and what is not
5. How eulogy and/or memorialization function within a particular context

---

Research Journal and Sketchbook Exercise 18

Locate several obituaries and analyze them, individually writing down all that you noticed, wondered about, and imagined.

Arrange the obituaries chronologically, then in alphabetical order, and then sorted by gender, age, geographic location, announced or assumed religious affiliation, etc.

Who wrote the obituaries?
Did they include pictures?

> How many words were used to convey the overview of the life?
> Did it include any genealogy details?
> Did you detect any humor being used?

Arts-Based/Arts-Informed/Arts-Infused Life Writing

Diaries

Diaries are a form of autobiographical writing, and most are meant to be shared and for the public. Diaries can be used for a wide variety of writing styles and voices, ranging from casual to formal. Diaries can be written in different modes: cathartic, confessional, reflective, subjective, objective, or descriptive. Different themes (for example, conflict between duty and desire or coming to terms with loss or self-affirmation) can be part of a diarist's writing. Some diaries function as collaborative texts and as a documentary of a family (Bunkers, 2002).

Voice in diaries as well as learning more about the diarist can be achieved by "mapping" the diary. This means examining the diary format and analyzing its link to the structure and format of the diary. This would include the number of lines allotted to each day and whether or not the author writes in the margins or circumvents the restriction by crossing out formatted dates. Diaries, far from the image of a locked journal, are now often written online and shared with a large readership (see for example, worldiaryproject.com, diarist.net/registry). This alters the relationship between the diarist and the diary and the readership that the diarist might have wanted preserved. Diary writing online can be a more public act rather than a private one even if traditional diarists often wrote for eventual public readership. (See www.michael-kimball.com/michael-kimball-writes-your-life-story-on-a-postcard/)

For a dynamic example of how to jumpstart an autobiographical or autoethnographic life writing project, Michael Kimball's book can be adapted in various ways.

Autobiographication

Autobiographication is another type of blending of life writing approaches within fiction.

In addition to the Carolyn Heilbrun example shared earlier, there are also new vistas within the comic book and graphic novel genres (Blanch and Mulvihill, 2013; Mulvihill and Blanch, 2015) and auto-biographical comics that emphasize the visual when narrating a life (El Refaie, 2012).

Research Journal and Sketchbook Exercise 19

1. Visit your local comic book store and select a comic book, or comic book series, and write about the ways they are arranged and what the visual adds to autobiographication.
2. Sketch or draw several panels as a representation of some aspect of the life you are writing.

References

Abbas, A., Ashwin, P., & McLean, M. (2013). Qualitative life-grids: A proposed method for comparative European educational research. *European Educational Research Journal, 12*(3), 320–329.

Arthur, P. L., Ed. (2014). Framing lives. Special issue. *Auto/Biography Studies, 29*(1), 1–9.

Backscheider, P. R. (1999). *Reflections on Biography*. Oxford, UK: Oxford University Press.

Bartleet, B.-L. (2013). Artful and embodied methods, modes of inquiry, and forms of representation. In S. Holman Jones, T. E. Adams, & C. Ellis (Eds.), *Handbook of Autoethnography* (pp. 443–464). Thousand Oaks: Left Coast Press.

Bartlett, F. C. (1932). *Remembering: An Experimental and Social Study*. Cambridge, UK: Cambridge University Press.

Belenky, M. F., Clinchy, B. M., Goldberger, N. R., & Tarule, J. M. (1997). *Women's Ways of Knowing: The Development of Self, Voice, and Mind* (10th Anniversary ed.). New York: Basic Books.

Berger, R. (2015). Now I see it, now I don't: Researcher's position and reflexivity in qualitative research. *Qualitative Research, 15*(2), 219–234.

Blanch, C., & Mulvihill, T. (2013). The attitudes of some students on the use of comics in higher education: Anthropology students' perceptions. In C. K. Syma & R. G. Weiner (Eds.), *Graphic Novels and Comics in the Classroom: Essays on the Educational Power of Sequential Art* (pp. 35–47). Jefferson, NC: McFarland and Company, Inc.

Bunkers, S. (2002). Whose diary is it, anyway? Issues of agency, authority, ownership. *A/B: Auto/Biography Studies, 17*(1), 11–27.

Collier, D. R., Moffatt, L., & Perry, M. (2015). Talking, wrestling, and recycling: An investigation of three analytic approaches to qualitative data in education research. *Qualitative Research, 15*(3), 389–404.

Creswell, J. W. (2013). *Qualitative Inquiry and Research Design: Choosing Among Five Approaches*. Thousand Oaks, CA: Sage.

Crotty, M. (1998). *The Foundations of Social Research: Meaning and Perspective in the Research Process*. Thousand Oaks: Sage.

Cunliffe, A. L. (2004). On becoming a critically reflexive practitioner. *Journal of Management Education, 28*(4), 407–426.

Denzin, N. K. (1989/2014). *Interpretive Biography*. Thousand Oaks: Sage.

Ellis, C. (2002). Being real: Moving inward toward social change. *Qualitative Studies in Education, 15*, 399–406.

El Refaie, E. (2012). *Autobiographical Comics: Life Writing in Pictures*. Oxford, MS: University Press of Mississippi.

Fine, G. (1987). *With the Boys: Little League Baseball and Preadolescent Culture*. Chicago: University of Chicago Press.

Forster. (2004). Rebecca's ghost. In M. Bostridge (Ed.), *Lives for Sale: Biographer's Tales* (pp. 52–56). London: Bloomsbury Academic Press.

Freedman, D., Thornton, A., & Camburn, D. (1988). The life history calendar: A technique for collecting retrospective data. *Sociological Methodology, 18*, 37–68.

Garrison, D. (1992). Two roads taken: Writing the biography of Mary Heaton Vorse. In S. Alpern, J. Antler, E. I. Perry, & I. W. Scobie (Eds.), *The Challenge of Feminist Biography* (pp. 65–78). Urbana: University of Illinois Press.

Greene, M. (1977). Toward wide-awakeness: An argument for the arts and humanities in education. *Teachers College Record, 79*(1), 119–125.

Greene, M. (1978). *Landscapes of Learning*. New York: Teachers College Press.

Haley, A. (1965). *Autobiography of Malcolm X*. New York: Grove Press.

Heilbrun, C. G. (1988). *Writing a Woman's Life*. New York: W.W. Norton & Co.

Heinrich, T., & Soeting, M. (2015). Beyond the subject. New developments in life writing. *European Journal of Life Writing, 4*, VCi–VCiii.

Hibbard, A. (2006). Biographer and subject: A tale of two narratives. *South Central Review, 23*(3), 19–36.

Irwin, R. L., Beer, R., Springgay, S., Grauer, K., Xiong, G., & Bickel, B. (2006). The rhizomatic relations of a/r/tography. *Studies in Art Education, 48*(1), 70–88.

Kimball, M. (2013). *Michael Kimball Writes Your Life Story (On a Postcard)*. Atlanta, GA: Publishing Genius Press.

Kridel, C., Ed. (1998). *Writing Educational Biography*. New York: Garland/ Routledge.

Leader, Z., Ed. (2015). *On Life-Writing*. Oxford: Oxford University Press.

Lee, H. (2015). "From memory": Literary encounters and life writing. In Z. Leader (Ed.), *On Life-Writing* (pp. 124–141). London: Oxford University Press.

Lieblich, A. (2004). Writing biography as a relationship. *Nashim: A Journal of Jewish Women's Studies and Gender Issues*, 7(1), 206–211.

Mantel, H. (2003). *Giving Up the Ghost: A Memoir*. London: Fourth Estate.

Mulvihill, T., & Blanch, C. (2015). Do serenity comics forecast our pedagogies of identity construction? In V. E. Frankel (Ed.), *Joss Whedon and Comics* (pp. 62–72). Jefferson, NC: McFarland and Co.

Mulvihill, T., & Swaminathan, R. (2012). Nurturing the imagination: Creativity processes and innovative qualitative research projects. *Journal of Educational Psychology*, 5(4), 1–8.

Mulvihill, T. M., Swaminathan, R., & Bailey, L. C. (2015). Catching the "tail/tale" of teaching qualitative inquiry to novice researchers. *The Qualitative Report*, 20(9), 1490–1498.

Nadel, I. B. (1984). *Biography: Fiction, Fact and Form*. New York: St. Martin's Press.

Robb, G. (2004). A narcissist's wedding. In M. Bostridge (Ed.), *Lives for Sale: Biographer's Tales* (pp. 11–14). London: Bloomsbury Academic Press.

Shortland, M., & Yeo, R. (2008). *Telling Lives in Science: Essays on Scientific Biography*. Cambridge: Cambridge University Press.

Stehlik, D. (2004). From "snowball" to "rhizome": A rethinking of method. *Rural Society*, 14(1), 36–45.

Swaminathan, R., & Mulvihill, T. (2017). *Critical Approaches to Questions in Qualitative Research*. New York: Routledge.

Taylor, A. (1992). *Annie Besant: A Biography*. Oxford University Press.

Thomas, W. I., & Znaniecki, F. (1918). *The Polish Peasant in Europe and America: Monograph of an Immigrant Group* (Vol. 2). Chicago: University of Chicago Press.

Tierney, W. (2002). Get real: Representing reality. *International Journal of Qualitative Studies in Education*, 15, 385–398.

Wheeler, S. (2004). Polar gap. In M. Bostridge (Ed.), *Lives for Sale: Biographer's Tales* (pp. 86–89). London: Bloomsbury Academic Press.

Wolff, G. (1979). Minor lives. In M. Pachter (Ed.), *Telling Lives: The Biographer's Art* (pp. 56–73). Washington, DC: New Republic Books.

4

EVALUATIVE CRITERIA
AND FINAL THOUGHTS

This chapter will include evaluative criteria used by qualitative researchers to guide high-quality projects, an overview of the debates about the need for evaluative criteria, and some final thoughts.

Evaluative Criteria for Life Writing Projects

Criteria used for evaluating qualitative research projects have been growing in sophistication and can be useful for those engaging in life writing projects. However, these may not always, in every case, find easy transferability or application in life writing projects. Yet, life writers can make good use of these frameworks as they are building and evaluating their own work. Below we offer some examples for consideration. Evaluative criteria help to establish overall trustworthiness and credibility of qualitative projects and there are several approaches scholars rely on, such as those provided by Lincoln and Guba (1985; 1990), AERA (2006), Schwandt, Lincoln, and Guba (2007), Tracy (2010), and Hughes, Pennington, and Makris (2012). Let's examine each briefly.

Lincoln and Guba (1985) developed a set of criteria to help establish the overall trustworthiness of qualitative inquiry projects, namely *credibility, transferability, dependability,* and *confirmability.* They later (1990) discuss four criteria specifically designed for case study reports, namely *resonance, rhetoric, empowerment,* and *applicability.* And then joining with Schwandt, they expanded the conversation to include not only criteria for trustworthiness but also for authenticity (Schwandt et al., 2007).

The American Educational Research Association's (AERA) *Standards for Reporting Social Science Empirical Research* (2006) convey two primary principles for research reports:

1. "Empirical research should be warranted; that is, adequate evidence should be provided to justify the results and conclusions."

(p. 33)

2. "Reports of empirical research should be transparent; that is, reporting should make explicit the logic of inquiry and activities that led from the development of the initial interest, topic, problem, or research question; through the definition, collection, and analysis of data or empirical evidence; to the articulated outcomes of the study."

(p. 33)

And later in *Translating Autoethnography Across the AERA Standards: Toward Understanding Autoethnographic Scholarship as Empirical Research,* Hughes et al. (2012) offered a very useful translation of the previously published AERA (2006) standards for autoethnographies and concluded by discussing the elements of a rubric that they contend will help researchers (reviewers and publishers as well) evaluate and effectively communicate the elements of autoethnography projects. They expanded upon AERA's standards to include more direct attention to qualitative research methodologies, namely autoethnography, which was often being methodologically challenged as it was making its way onto the life writing stage. In between these two standards documents came another document from AERA in 2009 meant to distinguish humanities-oriented educational research, American Educational Research Association's (AERA) *Standards for Reporting on Humanities-Oriented Research in AERA Publications.*

And finally, Tracy (2010) contributed eight "big tent" criteria: *worthy topic, rich rigor, sincerity, credibility, resonance, significant contribution, ethics,* and *meaningful coherence.* Tracy (2010) also argued for the pedagogical implication of using these criteria with novice researchers as they learn how to build and then evaluate their research projects.

Despite these attempts to formulate evaluative principles, or yardsticks, to measure quality, the evaluative criteria debates abound (Lather, 1993; Schwandt, 1996; Bochner, 2000), and there does not exist a unifying point of view about the need for, or usefulness of, evaluative criteria. Furthermore, these debates represent the shifting understandings of the power dynamics at play within any effort to create new knowledge. Experimental forms of life writing that traverse the borders of artistic expression are not always accepted by traditional academic communities as legitimate discourses of knowledge. Such criticisms may even come from within the life writing community. Duncan (2004), herself an autoethnographer, criticizes personal writing that is purely descriptive and does not include an analysis or theoretical grounding. Others, such as Bochner (2001), believe that we should not think of a narrative of a life as mere data to be analyzed and instead respect the story. Frank (2000) pointed out that the aim of the personal narrative is perhaps "not to engage [narrative] systematically, but to engage it personally" (p. 355). In such cases, we can argue that traditional criteria for judging overall worth do not align with experimental forms of expression. Bochner (2000) points out that emphasis on "criteria" separates the modernists from the postmodernists [and] the empiricists from the interpretivists" (p. 266), while some other scholars have suggested that we need to look at "literary criteria of coherence, verisimilitude and interest" (Richardson, 2000, p. 11). In other words, they are advocating that the questions we need to ask, the ones that will serve as the best guidelines of evaluation, would be: Does this experience resonate? Do I find this believable based on my own experiences? Ellis (2000) suggests further questions: "Can the author legitimately make these claims for [the] story? Did the author learn anything new about himself? Will this story help others cope with or better understand their worlds?" (p. 275).

Life writers can catch glimpses of these evaluative criteria debates in the literature, or drill down and study the intricacies to better determine the shape of the methodological literature, or borrow the tools offered by some in a more pragmatic way to help guide life writing projects. These explanations imploring researchers to be thoughtful and responsible members of the research community can be very instructive as projects are being designed and carried forward. And while on the micro-level they are operating in such a way to normalize (establish and monitor norms), on the macro-level they are important barometers of the social science tensions being worked through epistemologically, ontologically, artistically, and pedagogically.

Research Journal and Sketchbook Exercise 20

1. Locate a published life writing project. Select one set of evaluative criteria listed above and conduct your own analysis.
2. Develop a chart or table creating a cell for each evaluative criterion listed within one of the above frameworks and jot notes about the degree to which your current life writing project is attending to each.
3. Draw a sketch graphically representing how each individual criterion is connected to all the others in order to demonstrate the interactive nature of each of the criteria.

Research Journal and Sketchbook Exercise 21

1. Consider how you might create a Community of Practice (CoP) among life writers you know, or qualitative researchers you wish to encourage toward a life writing project, using the Wenger, McDermott, and Snyder (2002) CoP model organized around the following seven principles:
   A. Design for evolution
   B. Open a dialogue between inside and outside perspectives
   C. Invite different levels of participation
   D. Develop both public and private community spaces
   E. Focus on value

> F.   Combine familiarity and excitement
> G.   Create a rhythm for the community.
> 2.   Use Table 4.1 to fill in the boxes with your own planning notes for your life writing projects.

TABLE 4.1 Overview of Five Approaches to Life Writing

Project → *Types* *Stages ↓*	*Biography*	*Autobiography*	*Autoethnography*	*Oral* *History*	*Life* *History*
Topic/Problem/ Interest					
Epistemology/ Theoretical Perspective					
Literature Review					
Data Sources					
Data Analysis					
Organizing the Narrative/ Writing					
Conclusions/ Implications					

Final Thoughts: Pulling the Curtain

While there ought never be final thoughts about life writing projects, there are moments when the curtain must be temporarily pulled to signal an intermission, or an ending of the performance, yet we fully anticipate a continuation of exchanges among life writers and qualitative researchers. Continuations will necessarily involve new ideas, repurposed ideas, new actors, artists, thinkers, researchers, dreamers, all creating dreamscapes about how the process of engaging in critical life writing will benefit the creators and their audiences. Building Communities of Practice (CoPs), and other forms of collaboration that will support and extend the work of life writers, will help us all to courageously reimagine the possibilities for biography, autobiography, autoethnography, life history, oral history, and more forms of life writing yet to be further developed or newly created.

References

American Educational Research Association (AERA). (2006). *Standards for Reporting Social Science Empirical Research.* www.aera.net/Portals/38/docs/12ERv35n6_Standard4Report%20.pdf

American Educational Research Association (AERA). (2009). *Standards for Reporting on Humanities-Oriented Research in AERA Publications.* www.aera.net/Portals/38/docs/481–486_09EDR09.pdf

Bochner, A. P. (2000). Criteria against ourselves. *Qualitative Inquiry, 6*(2), 266–272.

Bochner, A. P. (2001). Narrative's virtues. *Qualitative Inquiry, 7*(2), 131–157.

Duncan, M. (2004). Autoethnography: Critical appreciation of an emerging art. *International Journal of Qualitative Methods, 3*(4), 28–39.

Ellis, C. (2000). Creating criteria: An ethnographic short story. *Qualitative Inquiry, 6*(2), 273–277.

Frank, A. W. (2000). The standpoint of storyteller. *Qualitative Health Research, 10*(3), 354–365.

Hughes, S., Pennington, J. L., & Makris, S. (2012). Translating autoethnography across the AERA standards toward understanding autoethnographic scholarship as empirical research. *Educational Researcher, 41*(6), 209–219.

Lather, P. (1993). Fertile obsession: Validity after poststructuralism. *Sociological Quarterly, 34*(4), 673–693.

Lincoln, Y., & Guba, E. G. (1985). *Naturalistic Inquiry.* Thousand Oaks: Sage Publications.

Lincoln, Y., & Guba, E. G. (1990). *The Paradigm Dialogue.* Newbury Park: Sage Publications.

Richardson, L. (2000). Evaluating ethnography. *Qualitative Inquiry, 6*(2), 253–255.

Schwandt, T. (1996). Farewell to criteriology. *Qualitative Inquiry, 2*(1), 58–72.

Schwandt, T. A., Lincoln, Y. S., & Guba, E. G. (2007). Judging interpretations: But is it rigorous? Trustworthiness and authenticity in naturalistic evaluation. *New Directions for Evaluation, 114*, 11–25. doi:10.1002/ev.223

Tracy, S. (2010). Qualitative quality: Eight "big-tent" criteria for excellent qualitative research. *Qualitative Inquiry, 16*(10), 837–851.

Wenger, E., McDermott, R. A., & Snyder, W. (2002). *Cultivating Communities of Practice: A Guide to Managing Knowledge.* Boston, MA: Harvard Business Press.

INDEX